A Chanticleer Press Edition

Wilderness

Michael Jenkinson

Rivers of America

Harry N. Abrams, Inc., Publishers,
New York

Photographs by Sam Abell, Dan Budnik,
Annie Griffiths, Wendell Metzen, Yva Momatiuk and
John Eastcott, David Muench, Boyd Norton,
George Silk, Charles Steinhacker, and Steve Wilson

For Walter, Evelyn and Robert Buell, on whose ranch, as a child, I first began to realize the subtleties of the natural world.

For Annetta Carter, who at the same formative period of my life, introduced me to the Sierra Nevada Mountains and the splendor of free-flowing water.

Michael Jenkinson

Preface

Naturalist Loren Eiseley once remarked: "If there is magic on this planet, it is contained in water." Having spent many of the most pleasurable days of my life rafting or canoeing wilderness waterways in the United States, Canada, and Mexico, I would agree. Every wild stream, lake and swamp is unique, possessing an ecosystem of plants and animals, a rhythm of flow and seasonal changes, subtleties of rock formations, banks, and islands which are all different from any other. Perhaps the most difficult task in preparing a book such as this is choosing which wilderness waterways to include, for, whatever the decision, a great many magnificent ones must be omitted.

The eleven waterways featured in this book were selected for their beauty and diversity. For much of its length, the Noatak River of Alaska winds across treeless Arctic tundra prowled by barren-ground grizzly bear. In the Big Bend country of Texas, the Rio Grande pounds its way through a remote series of scorched desert canyons inhabited by herds of javalina and an occasional mountain lion. Crocodiles in the Okefenokee Swamp, headwaters of the Suwannee River, lazily watch canoeists as they paddle through tunnel-like passages where tree branches meet overhead and masses of green and flowering vegetation seem to press on every side. The rapids of the Grand Canyon are considered to be some of the most violent navigable stretches of whitewater in the world; the Fraser River of British Columbia is famous for its huge whirlpools; yet in the Atchafalaya waterway of Louisiana, the current in many places is so gentle as to be almost imperceptible.

A number of the most magnificent waterways in North America are not conventional rivers. In this book, I have included chapters on the Atchafalaya, North America's largest river basin swamp; and the Boundary Waters Canoe Area, a vast maze of interconnecting streams and lakes in the North Woods, along the Minnesota-Ontario border.

The number of wilderness waterways is rapidly diminishing, often victims of unnecessary dams, pollution, and commercial development. Several of the rivers discussed in this book, such as the Upper Rio Grande, the Buffalo, and the Allagash, are now a part of the National Wild and Scenic Rivers system or are protected by other wilderness designations. The fate of others, including the Atchafalaya and the Noatak, are currently the subject of state and federal hearings; still others — the Fraser and the Hudson, for example — can yet be destroyed by dams or development.

Published in 1981 by Harry N. Abrams,
Incorporated, New York. All rights reserved. No
part of the contents of this book may be reproduced
without the written permission of the publishers

Composition by World Composition Services, Inc.,
New York
Printed and bound by Dai Nippon Printing Co., Ltd.,
Japan

Prepared and produced by Chanticleer Press, Inc., New York:
Publisher: Paul Steiner
Editor-in-Chief: Milton Rugoff
Managing Editor: Gudrun Buettner
Project Editor: Susan Costello
Natural Science Editor: John Farrand, Jr.
Production: Dean Gibson, Helga Lose, Ray Patient
Art Associate: Carol Nehring
Picture Library: Joan Lynch, Edward Douglas
Maps: Herbert Borst, H. Shaw Borst, Inc.

Design: Massimo Vignelli

Scientific Consultant: William H. Amos, St. Andrews School,
Delaware. Author: *Wildlife of the Rivers*

Library of Congress Cataloging in Publication Data
Jenkinson, Michael.
Wilderness rivers of America.

"A Chanticleer Press edition."
Includes index.
1. Rivers—North America.   I. Title
GB1212.J46   917.309693   80-20942
ISBN 0-8109-1776-9
Library of Congress Catalog Card Number: 80-20942

*Note: All illustrations are numbered according to the pages
on which they appear.
Pictures on pages 156–157, 160, 165, 169, 170–171, by George
Silk © 1974 Time-Life Books, Inc. from the American Wilderness*

*The wilderness waterways of North America display
the diversity of their landscapes — treeless spongy
tundra, glacier-hung mountains, hardwood forests,
deeply slashed desert canyons and freshwater swamps.
Each river as it flows from its source to the sea has
unique, often dramatic, characteristics. The Virgin
River of Utah (First Frontispiece), a tributary of the
Colorado, rushes over boulders as it emerges from a
narrow sandstone canyon in Zion National Park. Chill
water from melting snowfields (Second Frontispiece)
cascades into a gorge of the Fraser River of British
Columbia. Sometimes the more subtle features of a
river reveal haunting images, such as this reflection in
an eddy of Maine's Allagash River (Third Frontispiece).
[1–3. Steve Wilson. 4. Charles Steinhacker]*

Photographs by Sam Abell

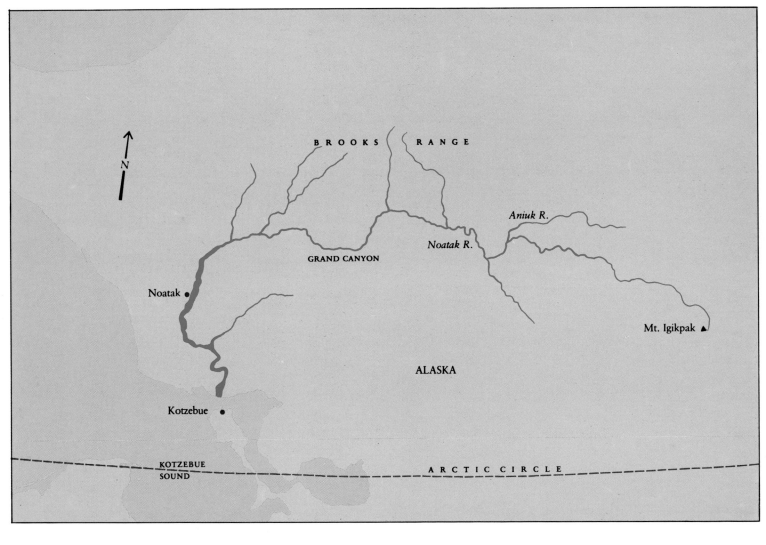

BROOKS   RANGE

N

Aniuk R.

Noatak R.

GRAND CANYON

Noatak •

Mt. Igikpak ▲

ALASKA

Kotzebue •

KOTZEBUE
SOUND

ARCTIC CIRCLE

0   80 Mi.

0   80 Km.

The Noatak

The Brooks Range of northern Alaska is thought to be the most remote mountain barrier in North America. Virtually uninhabited, it is a domain of windswept cliffs and tundra slopes. Until the completion of the Alaska pipeline, it was not crossed by roads or even well-used trails. A little more than half a century ago, forester Robert Marshall prowled the western Brooks Range, camping beside some of the chill rivers which drain it. He was moved to write: ". . . no comfort, no security, no invention, no brilliant thought which the modern world had to offer could provide half the elation of the days spent in the little-explored, uninhabited world of the Arctic wilderness."

The Noatak is as pristine a river as flows out of this high, lonely corner of the continent. It begins on the slopes of 8,510-foot-high Mt. Igikpak, the loftiest summit in the region. Gathering in a broad, U-shaped valley, the shallow current meanders through spongy tundra frequently split by gravel bars. For 435 miles the river pushes westward through wilderness before opening into Kotzebue Sound. The only settlement on the river, the Eskimo village of Noatak, has less than 300 inhabitants.

To reach the Noatak one can take a commercial flight to Kotzebue. From there, a floatplane can be chartered to fly to the highest navigable headwaters. Such a trip begins in a country of contrasts. Alpine spires soon give way to wide horizons broken only by clumps of dwarf willow. The numerous species of tundra plants are at once hardy yet fragile. Seeds of Arctic lupine that had been frozen in silt for 10,000 years can still produce healthy plants; on the other hand, damage to the delicate ground cover and thin soil layer usually leaves scars for centuries. It is often warm or even hot here in the summertime above the Arctic Circle; yet the water in the river remains a frigid 45 degrees.

When one stops paddling in this clear current and allows the boat to drift, the overwhelming impression is one of solitude, immensity, and the kind of silence that might have existed on the first day of the world. Before leaving the upper valley, it is worth hiking to one of the surrounding ridges for a view of the green and russet tundra as it sweeps up into the rocky bastions of the Brooks Range. Below, the narrow river winds between numerous deep blue ponds and lakes. It seems an austere landscape, yet life flourishes there.

Botanists marvel at the variety of plants in the Noatak drainage—a range of flora as broad as that of the entire Alaskan Arctic slope. When the surface soil thaws in late May or early June, a profusion of wildflowers bloom almost overnight—lupines, poppies, heather, rosebay, and mountain avens. Many of the tundra grasses seem as smooth and springy as a luxurious rug, yet there are also vast meadows of lumpy sedge tussocks. Some sedge tussocks, such as those of cottongrass, gradually build up out of a marshy surface, the younger plants thrusting out of the remains of older, dead grass. Instead of spreading at the base, the new growth often overlaps the old, causing the individual tufts to resemble some odd species of gigantic mushroom. Since an individual tussock may reach eighteen inches in height, a walk through this kind of growth can be tedious, but not impossible.

Beneath such plants and a thin layer of topsoil lies the permafrost—permanently frozen earth. Early-day prospectors, who panned gold along most of Alaska's drainages, including the Noatak, amused themselves around campfires with grisly tales about ingenious ways to dispose of the body of a "played-out" partner when digging a grave in the icy soil was impossible. Campers still have exasperating moments when they try to drive tent stakes into the frozen, unyielding ground. Most of the Noatak drainage basin receives less than fifteen inches of precipitation per year, scarcely more than many deserts. Yet, unlike dry country in more temperate climates, much of the snow and rain that does fall is retained in the form of ice that slowly melts during the long days of summer, nourishing the plants of the tundra cover.

After some fifty miles, the river gradually emerges from its valley and enters the Aniuk Lowlands, a vast shallow bowl where the river makes wide sweeping curves and channels over gravel bars. Long glacial moraines line the river in places, and there are rapids where the river cuts across them. The banks rise to a gently rolling tundra. Among the shrubs of dwarf dogwood, heather, and redbud are countless caribou antlers, shed by the thousands of animals that pour through Howard Pass at the head of the Aniuk River during their annual migration. This herd, estimated at 50,000 animals, calves on its summer pasture north of the Brooks Range and early in autumn fords the Noatak en route to the wintering range in the Kobuk and Selawik basins to the south.

The Noatak continues to grow, fed by rivers that tumble in over boulder-strewn mouths and by creeks that slip between sandy cutbanks. Up the Aniuk is whitewater to tempt the most intrepid kayaker; up another tributary is an untouched lake whose shores contain so many delicate and possibly
14 unique plants that botanists hardly dare to walk there.

Arctic terns wheel over the widening waters, occasionally divebombing past an intruder's ears if he has drifted too close to their nests. Monochromatic stretches of reindeer moss, pale as the felt of an old billiard table, are broken up by the brilliant colors of tundra flowers.

In some places, one can step directly from a canoe onto a parklike expanse of open tundra. Elsewhere, the river is lined with thick tangles of alder and willow. Eskimos use the sap of alder leaves to relieve the itching from mosquito bites. The willow is even more useful to them: They chew the inner bark for its nourishing sweetness, eat young buds and shoots in their entirety, and make baskets, fish traps, and snowshoe frames from strands of older, tough bark. Berry patches are everywhere—blueberries, cranberries, bearberries, curlewberries. Ripened under the long days of summer sun, the berries are large and surprisingly sweet. Early autumn cranberries and blueberries frozen on the vine are not only edible but also rich and juicy when they thaw in the spring, and bears, emerging from hibernation, fatten upon them.

Like most of the chill streams that originate in the Brooks Range, the Noatak and its tributaries teem with Arctic grayling, black-flecked, silvery fish with large, sail-like dorsal fins. Like trout, grayling favor cold, clear streams, although they are even more fastidious about the quality of their environment than are trout. In Arctic waters, grayling rarely grow to more than eighteen inches. They are sleek, swift swimmers that in the winter often travel long distances to find deep pockets where the stream never freezes all the way to the bottom.

An observant traveler is almost certain to notice some tracks of the barren-ground grizzly along the Noatak. Opportunities for seeing a bear or two are good, and the possibilities of coming face to face with one are not remote. Suddenly coming into close quarters with a grizzly is a profound experience, especially in this region where there is nothing to climb except dwarf trees that are shorter than the reach of the bear. It is a way of really knowing you are in the wilderness, quite thoroughly in the domain of undomesticated creatures. For all of their potential ferocity, the great hump-shouldered animals will usually amble away from the scent or sight of man. Yet grizzlies are intelligent and unpredictable; outdoorsmen sharply differ over the advisability of carrying guns for protection. Many non-hunters do not, despite the possibility of being mauled. I know of one Arctic voyager who effected a compromise between the two positions by carrying firecrackers in his pack. Although the explosions of the firecrackers once did send an overly curious grizzly rushing away from his camp, they were chiefly used to delight the Eskimo children and their parents.

Gradually, the broad expanse of the Aniuk Lowlands begins to be funneled by an abrupt spur of the Delong Mountains to the north and the Baird Mountains to the south. This is the Grand Canyon of the Noatak; not a gorge proper like the Grand Canyon of the Colorado, but a lovely 70-mile-long valley bordered by cliffs of endless variety. These escarpments finally crowd to the edge of the water, forming Noatak Canyon, a six-mile slot through which powerful currents swirl. Precipitous walls rise from 200 to 300 feet high. One has re-entered the world of trees. Dwarf spruces are scattered through the lower reaches of Grand Canyon, most of them no more than waist high. Barren-ground grizzlies walk over them to scratch their stomachs. In Noatak Canyon, stands of spruce become taller, denser, and more thickly clustered.

Noatak Canyon opens into the Mission Lowlands, where the river is dotted with mudbars and wooded islets. In addition to the innumerable Arctic ponds and lakes, the main channel is often flanked by sloughs. Mosquitoes seems to be especially numerous and persistent here, particularly in the early summer. One can minimize their depredations, however, by avoiding soggy campsites. The traveler is rarely bothered on the open river.

Another inhabitant of the Mission Lowlands is the celebrated whistling swan. It is a large, white bird of exquisite grace and beauty. As ice begins to form at the edges of the water in autumn, the whistling swans begin their long migration southward. Tagged whistling swans from the Noatak have been recovered in California, Utah, and Maryland. The Mission Lowlands are also a major nesting area for Canada geese, snow geese, and a variety of ducks. Moose, relative new-comers to this country, browse their way through dense willowbrakes. Although caribou have inhabited the Noatak River country for at least ten thousand years, local Eskimos did not begin to see moose until the early part of this century.

Low knolls, or pingos, ranging from 20 to 300 feet in elevation, rise symmetrically and abruptly from the flat tundra floor. Pingos begin as ponds which gradually fill with silt. When the silt freezes solid, the pressure of the permafrost beneath and around the former pond slowly pushes it upward into a mound.

The village of Noatak is perched upon a high bank above the river about midway through the Mission Lowlands. Like most Eskimo communities, it is a mixture of old and new. While most of the housing is of the prefabricated variety provided by the Bureau of Indian Affairs, there are also a number of traditional log dwellings. Some families rely upon snowmobiles for winter travel, others upon dog teams, and still others possess both. Here a snowmobile is both fast and efficient—until it breaks down a long way from anywhere. Snowmobiles consume gasoline that must be purchased with hard cash and costs more each month, but the more economical sled dogs eat salmon scooped from the river. Beside the river, salmon are dried upon poles in an age-old process. Outside the Community Hall, a dish antenna points at a satellite 22,000 miles away, facilitating telephone contact with the outside world.

Noatak was founded in 1908 by two Quaker missionaries from California. The village grew slowly around the nucleus of a federal school and a community church. The permanent population of Noatak is less than 300, and this fluctuates with the season, since these are a hunting and fishing people. Caribou is the mainstay of the villager's diet. They eat all of the animal—leaving only the entrails, bones, and hooves for the sled dogs to fight over. Winter clothing fashioned from caribou hides is warmer than anything purchased from the mail-order catalogues that find their way into the village.

The seining of salmon during the summer spawning runs is a major activity. Almost everyone has a hand in the fishing, as well as the cleaning, smoking, and

15

sun-drying. Skiffs propelled by outboards purr up and down the river between fishing camps. The period of the runs becomes a prolonged salmon feast, but most of the fish drawn flopping from the water are split up the middle, scored, and dangled from poles for smoking or sun-drying. Most of the sun-dried salmon will provide food for sled dogs over the long winter months.

In 1971 the federal government passed the Alaska Native Claims Settlement Act, which has profound implications for the Noatak villagers as well as the future of the entire Noatak River drainage. In the contiguous United States, most Indian lands were either taken outright or were procured through broken treaties. Seeking a just solution to the territorial claims of Alaska natives, the bill allocated forty million acres of land and a billion dollars to the sixty thousand Indians and Eskimos of Alaska. A clause in the bill also instructed the Secretary of the Interior to choose extensive scenic lands to be set aside for future generations as national parks, forests, wild river systems, and wildlife preserves. It is perhaps the most important conservation legislation in history.

Among the 80 million acres that were designated as preserves two years later was the 7.6 million-acre Noatak National Arctic Range, a wildlife refuge that encompasses most of the river's drainage. The headwaters would be in the new Gates of the Arctic National Park, while most of the land from twenty miles above the village of Noatak to the river delta would be owned by a native cooperative.

The recommendation to preserve the Noatak River came about, at least in part, from the report of botanist Stephen B. Young who after studying the region with other scientists concluded: "We feel that the Noatak Valley and the surrounding countryside afford one of the last opportunities in the United States, or for that matter the entire world, to set aside for the future a wilderness of such size, variability, and complexity that it functions as a complete ecosystem."

Below the Noatak village the river continues to flow at a broad, leisurely pace, slicing at cutbanks, constantly shifting its channels. In places the strong current swings against sweepers—trees that have toppled across the water from a cutbank. They pose a real danger, and many a canoe or kayak has been swept into them and capsized. The sky, the woods, and the water are often filled with birds. Owls, which the Eskimos use to make soup, call from spruce branches. During the spring, entire families from Noatak navigate this area in their boats, seeking gull eggs, which are as tasty as those of a chicken. In early autumn, hundreds of snow geese cloud the sky as they set off on a migration which will take them as far south as the Gulf of Mexico, 3,000 miles away. Sandhill cranes, also long-distance migrants, emit their weird, rattling cries as they flap to flight from sandbars. In addition to salmon and whitefish, the waters contain Arctic char, a colorful, hook-jawed member of the trout family.

The Noatak current pushes one's boat ever closer to the sea, past magenta fields of fireweed and past ravens hopping solemnly about on a gravel bar, maneuvering around the half-picked bones of dead fish. A voyage down the Noatak is not only an experience of solitude but of nightlessness. Even though the sun does set briefly, there lingers a pearly blue light over the land. You can read by it. After a while, traveling without a watch, you begin to eat, sleep, and stay on the river in terms of your own inner cycles. At first one is plagued with questions, such as: Is it time to make camp now? Have I slept two hours or eight? How can I date my log? But as anxieties of distant timetables begin to slip away, one of the most subtle yet intense meanings of running a river like the Noatak becomes apparent. For this sojourn, the myriad boxes of time and space we must build around ourselves in the world we come from can be thrown away. Intervals are changes in the pulse of this water. . . a shambling porcupine. . . shapes of clouds upon the land . . . one is as timeless as the river.

After the Noatak River passes between the Igichuk Hills in Lower Noatak Canyon, it broadens in places until it seems more like a lake than a river, and a stiff wind blowing off Kotzebue Sound may actually push a boat upriver. From the muddy mouth of the delta, where seabirds wheel and dive, it is a ten-mile paddle across Kotzebue Sound to the town of Kotzebue, termination for a voyage down a river worthy of preservation for our children and their children.

17–19. *Alaska's Noatak River, which drains more than 12,000 square miles of Arctic wilderness, loops its way out of the Brooks Range — the most remote mountain barrier in North America. Here, close to the headwaters of the Noatak, glacier-fed tributaries have merged to form a chill, shallow waterway which meanders through spongy tundra.*

Between the windswept crags of the Brooks Range and the Bering Sea, the 435-mile river flows past only one village — an Eskimo settlement of less than 300 people.

Tundra flowers such as the moss campion (above left) and the alpine saxifrages (above right) seem to bloom overnight, much like desert flowers in warmer climates. Although the permafrost, a core of frozen soils, often lies only inches beneath the surface of the tundra, precipitation is scant and plants must be hardy to survive. The moss campion has evolved stubby branches which catch sand and leaves, serving to trap precious moisture. Growth is directed toward developing the taproots. A plant may be 25 years old before it flowers profusely. The saxifrages, whose name means "rock breaker," often lift their pale jade flowers out of boulder cracks so barren of soil that the flowers appear to grow from the rock itself.

*A barren-ground grizzly
forages for berries along
the upper reaches of the
Noatak. Although smaller
than the brown bear
found along the seacoast
of southern Alaska, each
grizzly requires a hundred
square miles of habitat to
survive in the challenging
Arctic environment.*

*The action of water
against grass and sand
have created an endless
gallery of abstractions in
the upper Noatak drain-
age. A sprig of grass (left)
growing in a lake near the
headwaters takes on
sculptural, shamanistic
qualities against a pattern
of ripples. The almost
transparent current (right)
at river's edge shimmers
across a sandy shelf.*

23

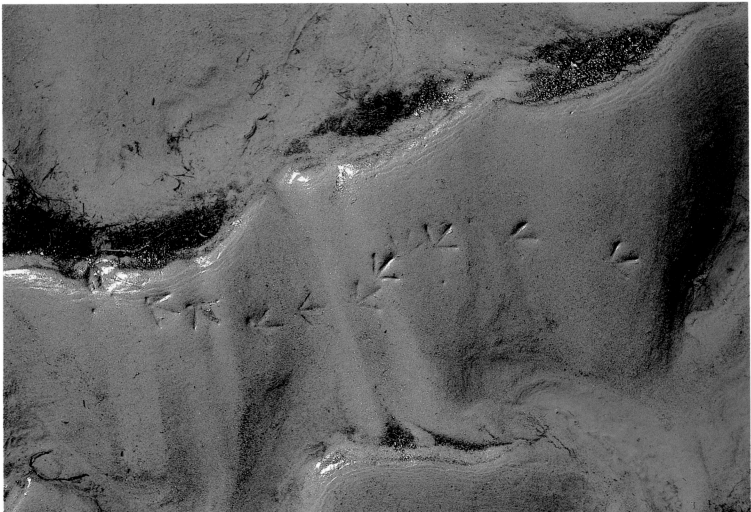

24

About 50 miles downstream from the Noatak's source the gallery of abstract views continues. Above left, sandpiper tracks imprinted on the sand and distinctive patterns (right) created from receding water.

26–27. *In the aftermath of a late afternoon storm, the sun highlights the chop of the Noatak above the entrance to a seventy-mile-long valley called the Grand Canyon of the Noatak. For most of this distance, cliffs lie well back from the river, but downstream at Noatak Canyon, a six-mile cleft, they rise directly from the water.*

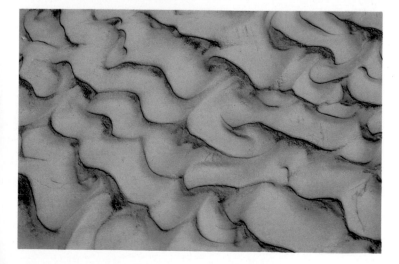

26

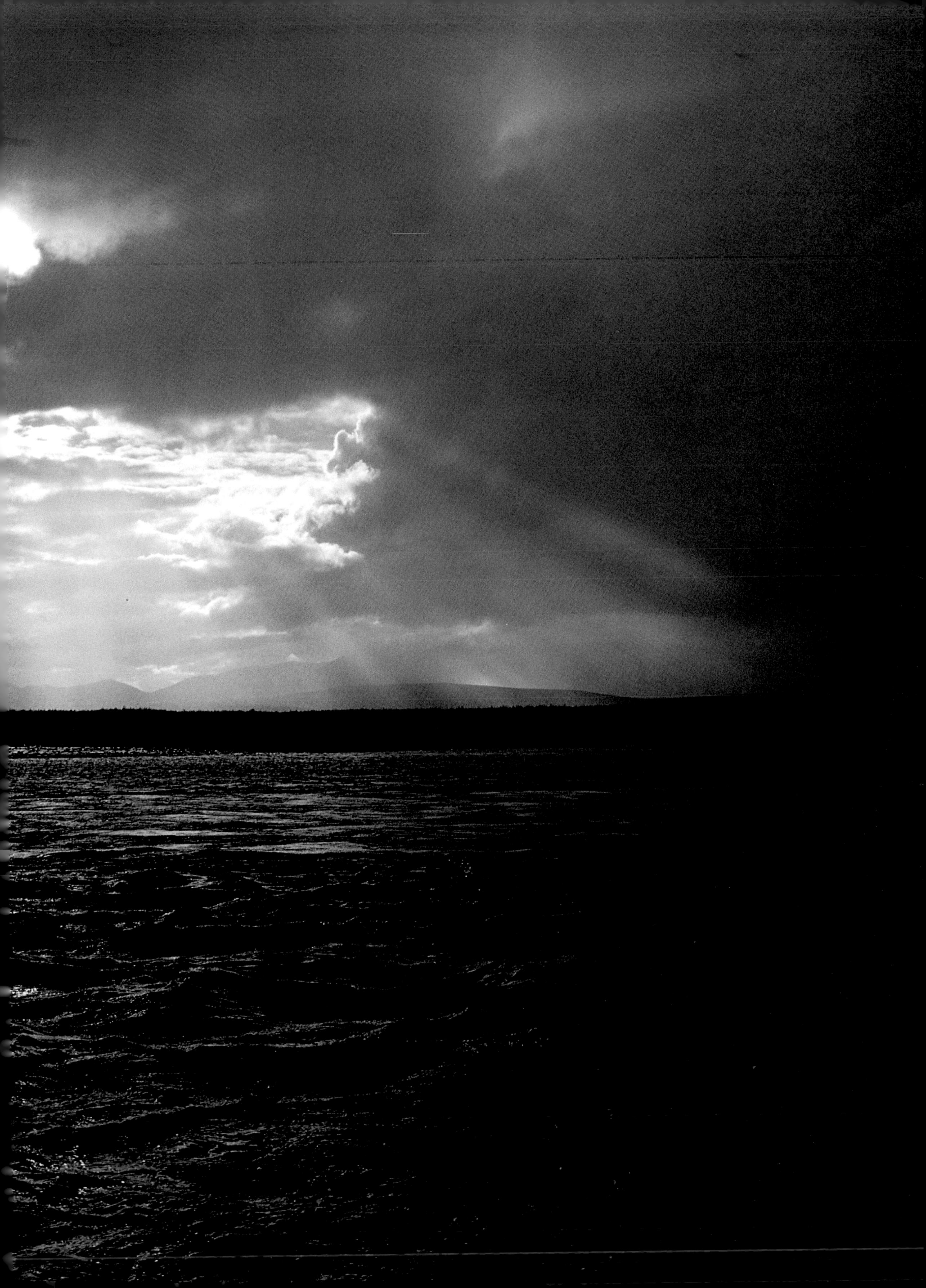

A lake above the Grand Canyon of the Noatak mirrors grass and a bank of clouds. Cottongrass in seed (below right) crowds the shoreline. The range of plants in the Noatak drainage is as broad as that of the entire Alaskan slope, and numerous flowers such as lupines, poppies, heather, and mountain avens bloom in the perpetual sunlight of the summer months.

30–31. *Rocky hills loom over the confluence of the Noatak and the Kelly rivers. A salmon run ascends the Kelly to spawn, and the confluence is a popular fishing grounds for the Eskimos of Noatak village. Fingerlike projections of dwarf spruce line the bank. For most of its length, the Noatak rolls through treeless tundra.*

A porcupine (left) shambles along the shore of the Noatak not far from the river's delta. Like most animals which inhabit this remote and rarely visited country, porcupines exhibit little or no fear of man.

An Arctic tern (above right) wheels over the muddy mouth of the Noatak Delta. The migrations of terns span immense distances. Once this young bird heads southward, it will fly to the Antarctic before returning to the Noatak region — a journey of some 20,000 miles.

A rainbow (below right) arcs over the shoreline of the Noatak Delta. Here, the river broadens in places until it seems more like a lake.

33

34–35. *The Noatak Delta at sunset. From this section of the lower river, whose shallow waters contain numerous sandbars, it is a ten-mile voyage across Kotzebue Sound to the town of Kotzebue.*

34

Photographs by Steve Wilson

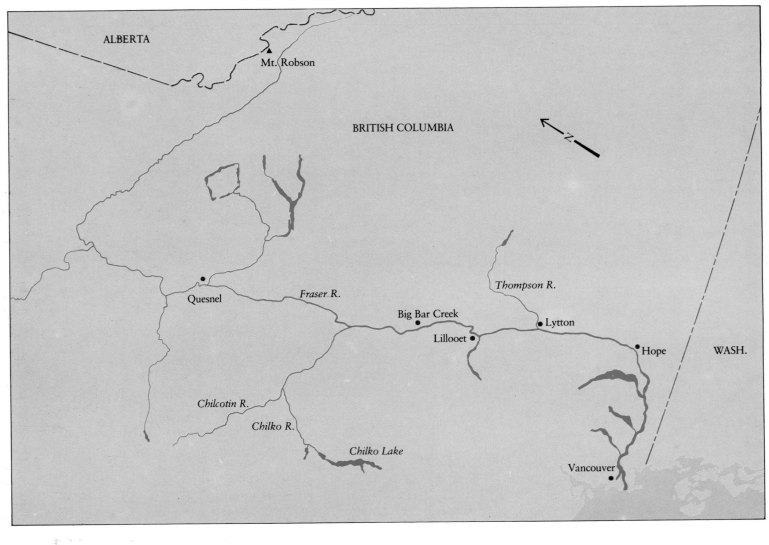

ALBERTA

▲ Mt. Robson

BRITISH COLUMBIA

N

Thompson R.

Fraser R.

Quesnel

Big Bar Creek

Lytton

Lillooet

Hope

WASH.

Chilcotin R.

Chilko R.

Chilko Lake

Vancouver

0   120 Mi.

0   120 Km.

The Fraser

In 1793, fur-trader Alexander Mackenzie attempted to reach the Pacific Ocean by following the Fraser River. Discouraged by fast water on the upper river, and Indian tales of violent rapids and monstrous whirlpools farther on, he trekked across the Coast Range on foot, becoming the first man to cross the North American continent north of Mexico. Fifteen years later, another fur-trader, Simon Fraser, managed to reach the mouth of the river which now bears his name, but not before abandoning his boats and inching along a precipitous cliff trail used by Indians. After a major gold strike on a tributary of the Fraser in 1861, a rough wagon road and later a railroad were blasted out of the cliffs of the Fraser River canyons. Traffic to and from the gold fields was brisk, yet one stretch of the river, more than 125 miles of water between Soda Creek and Lillooet, was untouched by this surge of activity. Steamboat captains deemed it unnavigable; roads and railroads bypassed it.

Today, from a wilderness standpoint this is the finest section of the river; it is still roadless and relatively wild. Canadian River Expeditions, based in Vancouver, conducts raft trips down this stretch during the summer months, and two years ago I made the trip with them.

After a spectacular flight over deep, slab-sided valleys, lofty waterfalls, and glaciers of the Coast Range, our float plane set down on Chilko Lake, headwaters of the Chilko River, a tributary of the Fraser. The lake is fifty miles long, yet in most places only a mile or two wide, its deep cerulean waters squeezed by ragged peaks and knife ridges. The upper end is remote and unfrequented. From the lakeshore, forests of Douglas fir and lodge-pole pine sweep upward into vast fields of snow as well as wind-raked, bare rock faces. Some years, in early summer, the pine pollen is so thick that it blows down the lake in a yellow cloud, filming the surface of coves and lagoons. The Homathko icefield sprawls back from some of the larger peaks such as Mt. Queen Bess and Good Hope Mountain, a mist-shrouded world where unnamed rocky horns thrust skyward out of glaciers. It is a twenty-five-mile-wide domain of silence, although far underfoot the ice is slowly pulverizing mountains and carving new valleys. Some of the glacial streams find their way into Chilko Lake. Franklyn Arm, a narrow bay, is milky with glacial silt, but it soon settles. The lake is over a thousand feet deep and so clear that on shallow shelves we could watch trout or dolly varden follow our lures.

Shortly after our float plane had landed on the lake, a motorized raft picked us up and transported us to Honeymoon Point, a grassy promontory. It is an idyllic campsite, with enough breeze or wind to blow bloodthirsty insects off course, yet enough gnarled Douglas fir to provide windbreaks. By early summer, Indian paintbrush, clusters of white yarrow, purple fleabane, and succulent wild onion have pushed up through the grasses, and wild roses as well as patches of fireweed give color to the shoreline.

We spent two days at Honeymoon Point, loafing, fishing, and exploring. I could cheerfully have lingered for two weeks or two months. Back in the woods, there are unexpected glades where streams trickle over mossy, lichen-covered rocks. Bald eagles make stick nests the size of wash basins on the tops of trees or on inaccessible ledges. Grizzly bear amble through the forest. Their muscled mass and rolling gait belies the swiftness of which they are capable. Here and there, visitors to this country will find huge tree boles which have been upended by grizzlies in quest of grubs. The great bears have been known to flatten full-grown moose. Coming upon a steep snowslope, they will often squat on their haunches and slide to the bottom. This region is believed to contain the largest concentration of grizzlies in North America.

Early on the morning of the third day, we headed down the lake, passing a large coffee-colored boulder. Frost had cracked and shaved the surface so that it bristled with delicate spikes. Across the lake, massive, chunky mountains loomed up from the water, the pale light accenting their upbent metamorphic strata as though revealing imperfect takes of God's own thumbprint. At a lodge at the end of the lake we changed from motor-powered rafts to paddleboats and entered the Chilko River. It is a fast, shallow waterway, and like Chilko Lake, transparent enough to see trout darting away. The mountains fell behind us as we began passing through forests of the Chilcotin Plateau. There were fewer fir trees now, but those we saw lifted high above the smaller lodgepole pines. Many of the firs had been charred by the fires which periodically sweep through this dry country: the lodgepoles are more likely to burn down while the thick firs become more fire-resistant with each conflagration they survive. There was a stiff breeze blowing downriver, and several times we startled flocks of mergansers, causing them to beat their way over us, their rust heads on graceful necks straining into the wind as if seeking its source. We floated past a moose with calf who regarded us lazily before loping away, and a six-point buck who flared his nostrils and snorted, perhaps in outrage, before wheeling off into the willows.

All along the Chilko River and later the Chilcotin River we drifted past small clearings with split-rail snake fences and deserted sod-roof cabins and barns — line camps for pioneer ranches or homesteads. It was like looking at old sepia photographs, so perfect in their setting that I always half expected to see a man in a buckboard approaching across bunch grass of the meadow, or a woman wearing a sunbonnet step out of the doorless cabin to scatter corn for chickens.

The upper Chilko River is swift, yet there are no rapids of consequence until it enters the mouth of Lava Canyon where it churns and boils for five miles through a layer of hard basalt. We portaged the canyon, although experienced river runners have rafted it, usually wearing rubberized wet suits as several rapids are back-to-back and the water is numbingly cold. We put in again where the Taseko River mingles its flow — ivory-colored from suspended glacial silt — with that of the clear Chilko. From here on, although the water would still be refreshing to drink, trout watching, or even catching for the most part, was over. We now boarded larger rafts equipped with rowing frames and engines. The current after the two rivers meet is fast-moving and authoritative, breaking savagely around sandbars and feeding into deep, swift channels which rush off through willow thickets. The country was becoming more open, with fine stands of cottonwood and quaking aspen. From time to time we would see kingfishers skimming over the water or popping in or out of tunnels in clay cutbanks which lead to their underground nests.

Maps show the Chilko River as a tributary of the Chilcotin River. The Chilcotin is, in fact, longer, but at the confluence the Chilcotin seems little more than a small side creek feeding into the broad and swift current of the Chilko. That night we camped on a grassy meadow with a herd of horses. One of the mares wore a bell around her neck. In the middle of the night I awakened as the bell clanked directly over my sleeping bag. The mare seemed to be trying to decide if my green bag was edible. Shortly before dawn, a flock of crows began raucously quibbling; moments later, I heard an agitated quacking of wild ducks. It seemed as if the two feathered species were arguing over something.

The country continued to change. After winding through a forested section known as The Goosenecks, we were now floating between sage and bunchgrass pastures, dotted with stubby, upright cactus scarcely bigger than a man's thumb. The hills south of the river were still covered with pines. The plateau to the north had eroded out into badlands, sand slopes, and the curious, isolated cones known throughout the West as hoodoos. Early accounts indicate that this region was once greener, a network of rills and ponds, before trappers depleted the beaver population in the last century.

Above Farwell Canyon we saw a flock of some thirty California Bighorn sheep stringing their way along a sandy apron, taking their time and turning to gaze back at us. Later we would see sheep peering over the edge of the escarpment at us, or poking their horned, bearded heads out from between grotesquely eroded hoodoos, like satyrs in some extravagant stage set. During the course of the afternoon we saw some 55 to 60 of these animals. A large wedge of plateau between the Chilcotin and Fraser rivers had been set aside as a sheep preserve and they have thrived.

Farwell Canyon is a sheer-sided gorge which squeezes the current of the Chilcotin into waves big enough to flip a misguided craft. Harry Marriott, pioneer cowpuncher in this region, described his first view of Farwell Canyon in his book, *Cariboo Cowboy*: "The river was sure aboiling down through that canyon, just arunning like the mill tails of Hell, and looking at it, I figured a man would never have a chance of ever getting out alive, if he ever got in there." We had a wet, exciting ride.

Logging trucks barrel their way across the one-track-wide, hundred-and-twenty-foot-high wooden bridge which spans the chasm, hauling logs felled in remote valleys and precipitous slopes to the sawmills of Williams Lake. About seventy percent of Canada's lumber comes from British Columbia. Some of the cottonwoods and firs in Farwell Canyon seem to grow out of the rock itself, leaning at precarious angles and supported by extensive systems of exposed roots. The gauzy nests of tent caterpillars hung from some of the cottonwood twigs, stirred like phantoms in the occasional breeze.

Our last camp on the Chilcotin was at the head of Big John Canyon, named for John Mikes, founder of Canadian River Expeditions. Some of us hiked about a mile upriver in order to float the fast water back to camp in life jackets. At the edge of a broad meadow, we startled a sleek, glossy black bear who let out a whoof and crashed off into the undergrowth. Through Big John Canyon, the Chilcotin charges down into the deeper trench of the Fraser River. The next morning we headed through the canyon, our rafts tossed about like chips in the wildest whitewater of the entire run — Railroad Rapids. The rapids, named by approaching boatmen who likened its roar in the distance to the sound of a steam engine, was created five years ago by a massive landslide.

The Fraser is a huge, rolling flow, tawny with suspended silt which hissed beneath the rafts. Spring floods can be awesome. In 1972 the Fraser crested at 315,000 cubic feet per second, more than twelve times the maximum volume of the Colorado River.

This can be frigid country in the winter — cold snaps of forty degrees below zero are not uncommon. Yet summertime temperatures can push up to one hundred and ten degrees, and the canyon has an appropriately scorched look about it: sandy beaches, sage flats, leaning pulpits of dark rock, badlands, and lava flows. I spent much of my time in the water, floating alongside the raft, or, in faster sections, scooping up hatfuls of water to dump over my head. Floating a hot canyon on a cold river is downright sensual; it can be likened to becoming hungry every fifteen minutes and having the perfect food at hand to satisfy it.

Each year in these waters, salmon spawning takes place. Battling their way upstream against strong currents, sometimes for hundreds of miles, they persist until they reach their spawning grounds. There, the female thrashes a nest in gravel and deposits her eggs. The male fertilizes them and, soon after, the battered couple dies or manages to struggle to sea. For three months the young salmon incubate under four to ten inches of gravel before hatching. They remain as fry in the gravel until they have consumed the food in their yolk sac, and then emerge to reside in the stream until they are about six inches

39

long. Then, those which have not become meals for trout, or other predators, begin their long journey to the sea.

Since Farwell Canyon on the Chilcotin we had been running through or close to sections of the historic Gang Ranch, an empire of more than a million acres — one of the largest cattle ranches in the world.

The headquarters are well back from the Fraser, yet from time to time we would beach to examine abandoned log cabins which had housed cowhands, miners, homesteaders, or all of them at one time or another. The men who lived in these cabins were isolated for months of the year. Some of them preferred it that way. Harry Marriott recalled an old fellow named Charlie Jones, who rarely had visitors, and was taciturn and nervous as a cat around a strange dog when he did. He always slept with a forty-five caliber revolver under his pillow. He once told Marriott: "You know, I just don't want nobody to talk to me, Harry. If anyone talks to me it just gets me right off my chain of thoughts, and I don't like it worth a damn." Other men generally counted the days until they could go into the nearest settlement for conversation, drinks, women, games of chance, and general celebration.

The ferry at Big Bar Creek has been ingeniously designed so that wheels on overhead cables allow the strong current of the river to push it from one shore to the other. The ferry operator's job is only slightly less lonely than that of a lighthouse keeper, since the dirt road on the west bank of the river frays out to isolated ranches and timber holdings. Hunting season is the only time of the year when there is appreciable traffic on the road. The ascending, grassy country to the west of Big Bar Creek has a curiously rumpled appearance from the debris pushed ahead of long vanished glaciers. We now glided into Chisum Canyon, where high canyon walls constrict the river so that it surges back and forth, erupting into huge, swirling boils. As the Colorado River in the Grand Canyon is famous among rivermen for the ferocity of its rapids, so this section of the Fraser is justifiably honored for its whirlpools. We skirted a whirlpool in Chisum Canyon which was thirty feet wide: its madly spinning vortex was as deep as the average man is tall. Motors are essential here. Using

only oars, a raft could spin or be locked in an eddy for hours or even days.

Most of the abandoned dwellings on the Fraser are little more than lean-tos or dugouts. At Watson Bar, however, a huge slope-roofed barn and a large house dominate a meadow above the river. Untrimmed fruit trees are scattered about. I sampled an apple from a branch close to the house and found it slightly tart, but juicy. The farm had belonged to a man named McDonald, but when the creek he used for irrigation went dry, he had little choice but to move away with his family. Inside the house, which must have taken hundreds of hours of back-breaking labor to build, I found the walls covered with newspaper, commonly used on the frontier for wallpaper; a horse collar, a broken bedframe, and, hanging next to the front door as if placed there only hours before, a child's ice skates.

We floated on, past the windowless miners' shacks of abandoned China Bar, past a placer mine where in recent times three men had extracted millions of dollars worth of gold in three years and through the huge waves of Powerline Rapids. We entered Moran Canyon, whose whirlpools rival those of Chisum Canyon, where cliffs drop for 2,000 vertical feet into the water. In one narrow gap, the river is 300 feet deep. Sturgeon weighing close to a ton glide through eddies far beneath the surface. Based upon current scientific evidence, the sturgeon lives longer than almost any other animal. Fraser River sturgeons are occasionally caught with huge, hand-forged hooks which are baited with whole chickens.

We left the river close to the town of Lillooet, the majority of whose inhabitants are Indians who net salmon from the river much as their ancestors did. Beyond Lillooet, the Fraser rushes through other spectacular canyons, breaks into other formidable rapids. Yet the wilderness river ends here; for the rest of its journey to the sea it is flanked by road or railroad, or both.

To participate in a trip down the Chilko, Chilcotin, and Fraser rivers is a voyage from a world of glaciers and conifer forests to a canyon of sage, bunchgrass, and cactus. Few river journeys anywhere can offer such diversity in such a short span.

41

*Snow gradually melts out
of a willow thicket close
to the headwaters of the
Fraser River in Mt.
Robson Provincial Park,
British Columbia. After
winding to the northwest
through hills covered with
spruce and birch, the river
swings abruptly to the
south where a series of
deep canyons splits the
interior of the province.*

Chilcotin, the spring floods of the Fraser can be awesome. In 1972 the Fraser crested at 315,000 cubic feet per second — more than twelve times the maximum volume of the Colorado.

California newts (above right) living in Fraser River country breed in ponds but usually dwell in small caves or rotting logs or beneath stones. They are strong burrowers and feed upon grubs, slugs, worms, and insects.

Resembling some bizarre, beached sea creature, a brown salamander (below right) reclines in damp leaf litter. Like California newts, brown salamanders are widespread throughout the Fraser River drainage.

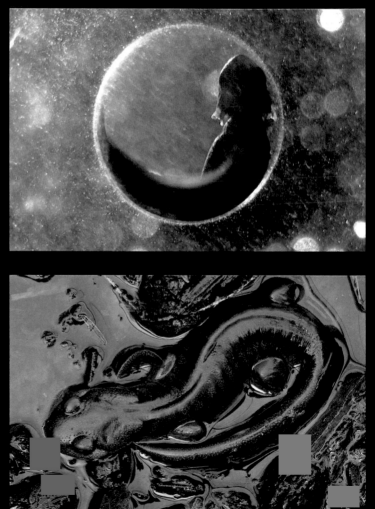

44

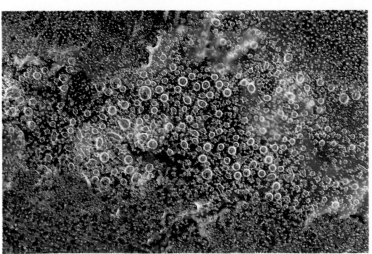

Water rushes into the Fraser River Canyon in the precipitous section between Yale and Hope. At above left, the showy blossoms of pearly everlasting lift beside a strand of falling water. Spring floodwaters (left) wash over a mossy boulder, and a rampaging creek (above) spurts through rock walls overhung by western red alder. At Hell's Gate, just north of this part of the canyon, the huge volume of the river bursts through a gap only 120 feet wide.

46–47. *Morning summer sun casts a rusty hue over the Fraser River between Quesnel and Williams Lake. In 1793, fur-trader Alexander Mackenzie attempted to follow the Fraser to the Pacific Ocean but soon became discouraged by rapids and reports by Indians of deep, impassable canyons to the south. Mackenzie reached the Pacific by an arduous overland route, but fifteen years later another fur-trader, Simon Fraser, managed to trace the river to its mouth at the site of the present-day city of Vancouver.*

47

48–49. *A great blue heron, a species found all along the Fraser, eyes the water's edge in hopes of spotting one of the fish, frogs, or large aquatic animals upon which it feeds. When prey is located, the heron swiftly stabs at it with its long, sharp beak.*

50–51. *Sockeye salmon gather below a rapids on the Thompson River, a tributary of the Fraser. Every summer, vast numbers of salmon leave the ocean to fight their way up the fierce currents of the Fraser River and its tributaries, drawn by a mysterious need to spawn in the precise shallow streams of their birth.*

Some salmon may travel for more than two months and cover 800 miles, rarely resting and never feeding. Although the salmon are able to leap their way up thunderous rapids, many die of exhaustion before reaching the spawning grounds. Those females that survive the ordeal lay hundreds of thousands of eggs in gravel beds; those males that have endured

fertilize them. Most of the battered parents-to-be then die. The following winter the fry are hatched, and, upon maturity, will make their own journeys to the sea.

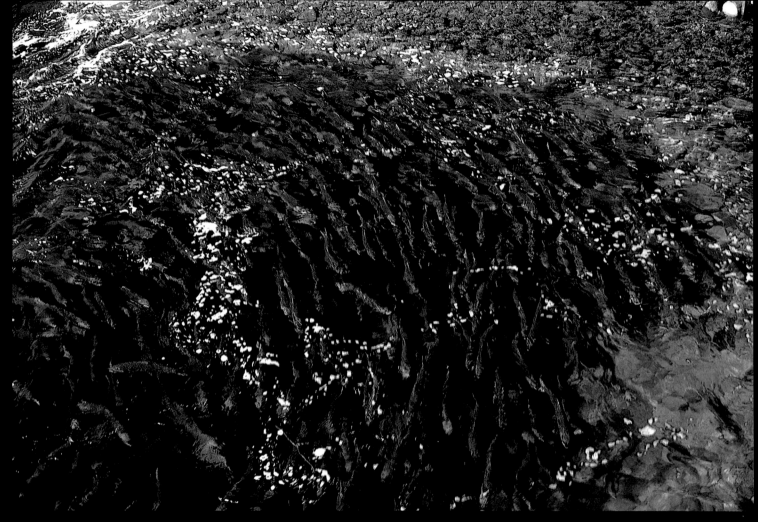

52–53. *Once the Fraser has cut through the spine of the Rocky Mountains in a series of slab-sided canyons through which the water boils and spins, it broadens and gentles as it swings westward to the Pacific. Here, Big Leaf maples overhang a leisurely current near the town of Agassiz.*

54–55. *Close to the mouth of the Fraser a mew gull glides over low swells of the Georgia Strait. The Fraser and its tributaries such as the Chilko and Chilcotin rivers pass from empires of glacier and thick conifer forests into dry canyons before slipping through parklike meadows and stands of hardwoods to the sea.*

54

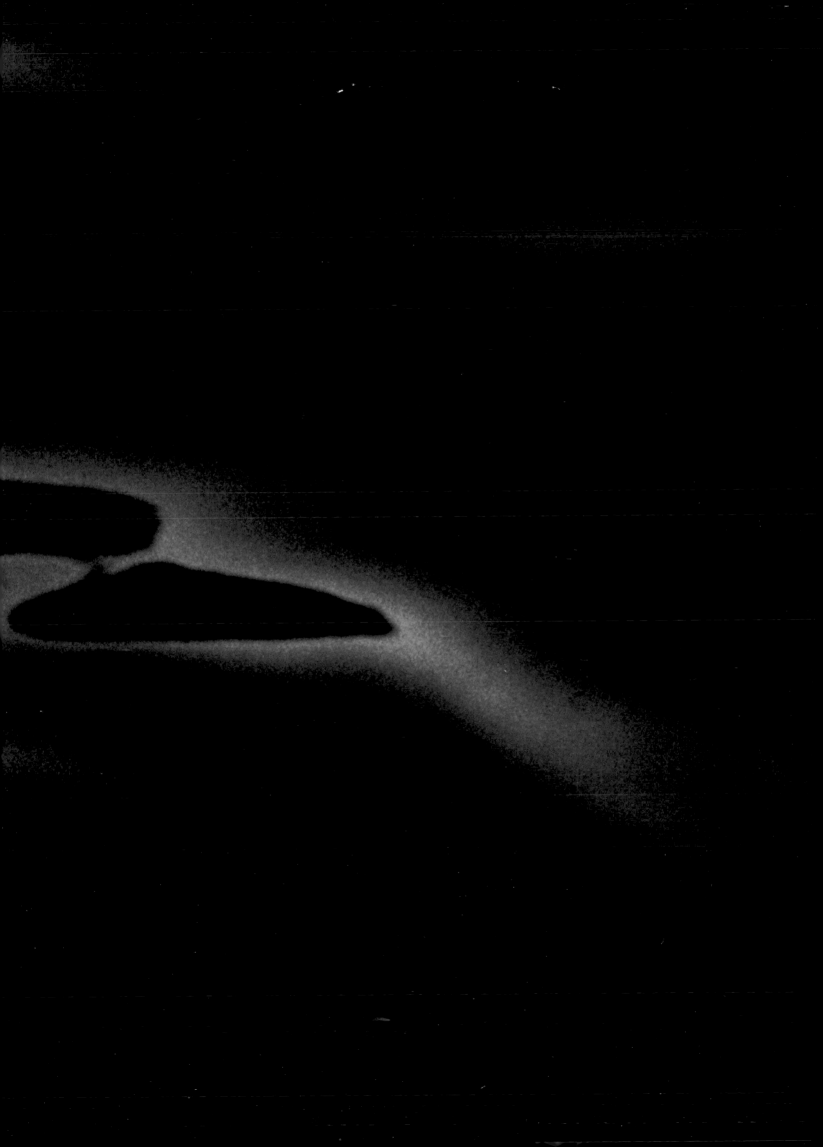

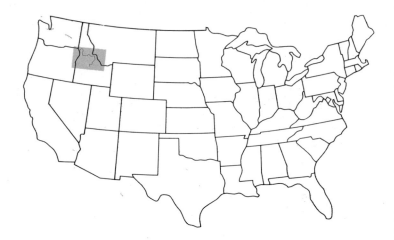

Photographs by Boyd Norton

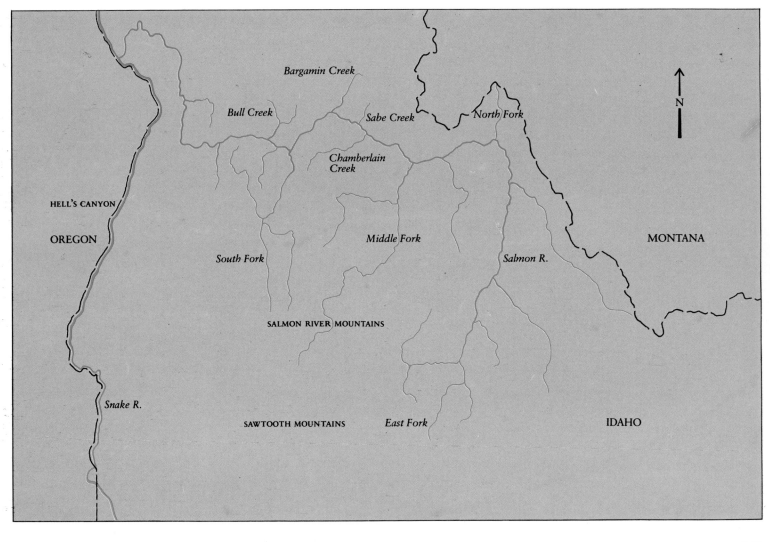

Bargamin Creek

Bull Creek

Sabe Creek

North Fork

Chamberlain
Creek

HELL'S CANYON

OREGON

MONTANA

Middle Fork

South Fork

Salmon R.

SALMON RIVER MOUNTAINS

N

Snake R.

SAWTOOTH MOUNTAINS

East Fork

IDAHO

| 0 | | 80 Mi. |
| 0 | | 80 Km. |

The Salmon

In 1804 two determined men led a party into the vast wilderness of the upper Missouri River, exploring hundreds of miles of unknown country in an effort to find an overland route to the Pacific. They were Captain William Clark and Meriwether Lewis.

Once they had crossed the Continental Divide they planned to float down a westward-flowing river into the Columbia. In their journals they noted that a Shoshoni chief had described the river ahead as: "obstructed by sharp pointed rocks and rapidity of the stream such that the whole surface of the river was beat into perfect foam as far as the eye could reach..." Clark, guided by another Shoshoni, proceeded for fifty miles down the Salmon River, a waterway that nineteenth-century frontiersmen would call the "River of No Return." He was appalled to find fierce rapids and steep hills, which could make portage arduous if not impossible. When his guide told him the river beyond rushed over even larger rapids and the walls of the canyon were "like the side of a tree straight up," he abandoned his plans for descending the river. The expedition would eventually reach the Columbia by another route.

The Salmon River begins high up in the rugged Sawtooth Range and the White Cloud Mountains, clusters of high, weathered peaks. This is a domain of abrupt, glaciated rock, lush meadows, and innumerable lakes and ponds. Swift tributary streams twist their way down wooded canyons and soon merge into the main river, which loops northward through the Salmon River Valley, where cattle graze knee-deep in grassy pastures separated by zigzag lodgepole fences. At the village of North Fork, the river swings to the west and begins to churn through a boulder-strewn canyon which is a thousand feet deeper than the Grand Canyon of the Colorado. Some one hundred million years ago a prodigious mass of granite intrusion buckled up an area of central Idaho some 250 miles long and 90 miles wide; to breach it, the Salmon gradually cut its way through the core. The granite cliffs and steep wooded slopes of the canyon rise thousands of feet to a vast, high empire of roadless wilderness — thick forests of fir, spruce, and pine broken by numerous lakes and meadows; towering peaks such as Bighorn Crags, a remote cluster of monuments and spires which stab up to over 10,000 feet in elevation. Countless chill streams wind through this high country, some of them all but entirely camouflaged from the air by dense foliage. They descend rapidly to the Salmon, white water rushing between rocks or twirling in deep pools where rainbow trout feed at twilight.

In places, ancient lichen-stained rockslides swoop down to the river's edge. Webbed with hackberry vines and sprouting spiky Devil's Clubs and other shrubs, they seem eternally passive. Yet within a few years, a century, or tens of centuries, the work of frost and seepage will have subtly shifted the mass until one day, perhaps during a rainstorm, the inertia will give way to gravity, and hundreds of tons of rock and rubble will crash into the river, partially choking it. Subsequently, over the years, the river's thwarted current will push and pry at the rocks, seeking to roll them aside or downstream, to break and reduce them until the river rages over what boulders remain — in other words, it will have become a rapids.

There are numerous rapids on the Salmon, ranging from lively riffles to roaring giants like Big Mallard, a wild jumble of waves and treacherous holes, or Chittam Creek Rapids, where in high water the entire river seems to smash directly into a face of rock on the left bank. This careening whitewater which deflected the Lewis and Clark expedition and has drowned a good many people since, has now become a major reason for coming to the Salmon. Each summer numerous rafts are inflated at Cache Bar, the customary starting point for a voyage down the River of No Return. Expert rafters and kayakers, who must obtain a permit from the Forest Service, head downriver on their own. The majority of people who travel the river do so with commercial outfitters, whose rafts are rowed by professional boatmen. There is little margin for error on the Salmon. Here and there beside the river, wrecked wooden river boats lie broken and deformed against rock and sand. For a time, the remains of a rubber raft stirred in an eddy on the Middle Fork like a dying water creature.

The Shoshoni Indians called the river Tom-Agit-Pah (big fish water). Countless Chinook, largest members of the salmon family, migrated up the river in the summer to spawn. The Shoshoni speared the magnificent red fish as they hurled themselves up fastwater shallows or rested in eddies. The great Chinook migrations up the Salmon River are a glory of another era. Heavy fishing and pollution on the Columbia have taken their toll, as well as intensive logging on the South Fork of the Salmon, which resulted in silt washing into the river and burying gravel spawning nests. Still, each year a number of fish continue to fight their way up the fast water of the canyon to spawn in brooks close to the Continental Divide.

Like the salmon, steelhead ascend the river to spawn as they have for centuries. After laying their eggs, these graceful silver-blue trout return to the ocean. Steelhead

may weigh more than twenty pounds, although most are less than half this size. Although its size and its migrations to and from the sea would seem to indicate otherwise, the steelhead is actually a rainbow trout. Rainbows thrive in the Salmon River and its Middle Fork, as well as all of the side streams flowing into it. Three decades ago a fisherman caught 280 trout on a five-day drift down the Middle Fork, releasing most of them from a barbless hook. Since then, the Middle Fork has become a victim of its own fame; so many fishermen have tested their flies upon it that certain side streams now yield better results.

During a layover on a raft trip down the Middle Fork, some friends and I worked our way up one of these steep, bushy creeks in a wispy pre-dawn mist. For a time, songbirds were so clamorous and the trout so elusive that we suspected collusion. Once the fish began to strike, however, they did so avidly, and by the time sunlight had slipped down the opposite canyon wall to the river we hunkered around the coals of a small fire where a feast of trout browned upon spits of sharpened willow twigs. Young rainbows and cutthroat trout are an important link in the food chain of the Salmon River country, providing meals for otter, mink, osprey, and the occasional enterprising raccoon or black bear. The trout feed extensively upon rust-colored stoneflies, which in turn obtain nourishment from green algae and bark fungus.

The rapids-torn Middle Fork has long been a favorite of river-runners. It appears that Harry Guleke was the first man to navigate the fast, rocky stream. He later remarked: "Sometimes I was on the raft and sometimes I was under it. But I was never afraid. And until a man is afraid, he'll be all right." The Middle Fork, always lively, can be highly dangerous in a year of high water. During a single week in the summer of 1970, four men were drowned. Yet most parties, if experienced or guided by experts, navigate the more than eighty rapids of the river without mishap.

The boil of fast water brackets quiet stretches where the river slips placidly between strands of massive Douglas fir and tall, supple ponderosa pine. In such places one drifts lazily past ever-changing banks. On occasion, one can spot quail or grouse picking their way through tangles of Oregon grape and the blossoms of lupine, which rise in blue and purple spires. Golden eagles circle high overhead, riding thermals from one canyon slope to the other. Once, at the foot of one short, choppy rapids, I briefly glimpsed what appeared to be a gray, feathered tennis ball plopping into an eddy. It was an ouzel, a bird that might have been created by Lewis Carroll. Although the ouzel has clawed rather than webbed feet and a stubby pointed beak, it feeds mostly on insect larvae in streams and rivers. From the shore, ouzels bob their heads into the water. If pickings are slim, they dive to the bottom of the river. Tiny sheaths plug their nostrils and transparent, protective lids slip over their eyes. Not able to swim, the ouzels walk along the bottom. If the current is too swift, they fly underwater to a less turbulent place, or back to the surface. Most birds favor dry locations for nest building. The ouzel prefers damp and noisy homesites such as ledges beneath waterfalls. Using fresh moss, the birds build elegant structures in the shape of a beehive. When the ouzel does take to the air, it invariably follows the course of the waterway.

At several places along the Salmon, one finds pictographs depicting birds, animals, and other highly stylized shapes. Like pictographs elsewhere in America, they were probably ceremonial in nature, made before or after a hunt as well as other important events. Many of them were made with red ocher — iron oxide stain — and they still stand out vividly against the buff rock upon which they are painted. Indians were living in the Salmon River Canyon 8,000 years ago. At many ancient campsites, archaeologists have found mounds of mussel shells, apparently a popular food. There are still plenty of freshwater mussels in the Salmon — you can feel for them with your toes and then root them out.

Weathered granite walls line much of the canyon. Rocky Mountain sheep wander across the cliff faces, nonchalantly balancing upon minute knobs of rock and occasionally leaping more than ten feet from ledge to ledge. Protected from most predators by their almost vertical environment, and now forbidden to human hunters, the sheep's most persistent enemy is the parasitic liver fluke. During rutting season, the rams rear back on their hind legs as if in an odd dance before smashing

their great curled horns together. Unless the battle is on the edge of a precipice, the loser eventually walks away. For rutting elk of the area, on the other hand, both contestants sometimes face death when their antlers become inextricably entangled . The sight of two elk skeletons still attached by locked antlers is one of the most haunting in the wilderness.

Visitors to the Salmon River Canyon often see Rocky Mountain sheep if they scan the rocks diligently; they are less likely to catch a glimpse of mountain goat as these equally agile animals tend to live higher up, on the crags and peaks which thrust above the canyon rims. Grizzly bear, once plentiful throughout western North America, have all but been annihilated in a century and a half. Less than two hundred of these magnificent solitary animals are left in the United States, and perhaps twenty of them wander the lonely reaches of central Idaho.

In spite of the rocky nature of the Salmon River Canyon, which caused one early-day settler to claim that the Lord had created it with a hatchet, the bottom of the canyon as well as many of the slopes are thickly forested. Stately Engelmann spruce are found all along the river. In autumn their large brown cones scatter black-winged seeds. On the slopes, ponderosa pine and Douglas fir give way to yellow pine as the canyon cuts deeper into new climate zones. In places, especially up side creeks, thick tangles of growth beneath the conifers make passage difficult if not impossible. In addition to the ubiquitous willow there is dogwood, whortleberry, chokecherry, serviceberry, and a variety of mosses and ferns. Huckleberry patches running to several acres ripen by August, a time of feast for black bears. When eluding a hunter, even large bears can slip through the woods with an eerie lack of noise, but a bear in a huckleberry patch makes a terrific racket.

In contrast to the mountain country around them, the canyons of the Salmon River and its Middle Fork usually have mild winters. It can be downright hot in the summer. During the Sheepeater War between the U.S. Army and the Tukuarika Indians, Captain Ruben Barnard and a detachment of troops descended into the gorge carved by the Middle Fork. He noted in his diary that "within a distance of ten miles we have come from ten feet of snow to roses and rattlesnakes." During the hard winter of 1861, the mining camp of Florence was completely cut off from the outside world by snow which lay ten feet on the level. It was not until May that a pack train floundered through the drifts to bring desperately needed provisions. In the depths of the nearby Salmon River Canyon, bunchgrass was already several inches high, berry bushes were leafing out, and early wildflowers — spring beauty, yellow bell, and buttercup — were in bloom.

The mild climate was not lost upon the men and women who built cabins on scattered benches along the river in the early days, and many of these settlers planted trees and gardens. In 1925 Frank Lantz floated down the river on a skow as far as Gunbarrel Rapids where his boat upset and he was knocked unconscious. He recovered in an eddy, hiked back to the town of Salmon for more provisions, and returned to the Rapids to build a cabin out of the boards of his broken boat. Later he planted an orchard of eighty trees: apples, peaches, plums, pears, and apricots. There were hermits like Earl Parrot, who constructed a cabin high above the Middle Fork which was only accessible by crude ladders set against walls of sheer rock. During the long winters he would, in effect, hibernate, sleeping as much as twenty-two hours out of twenty-four. On the other hand, Jack Killum and his family built their wilderness cabin right across the Salmon River trail, with doors on either side, so anyone passing through would almost be obligated to accept their hospitality.

As might be expected in such a lonely setting, many of the people who lingered there approached life with a unique sense of style. Fritz Music, a German miner, lived in a rock house built by Chinese miners and wore stovepipes on his legs for rattlesnake protection when he walked to Riggins for supplies. Sylvan Hart, better known as Buckskin Bill, still lives on a remote crook of the Salmon, where in a cluster of buildings he constructed from rock and homemade cement he smelts and refines copper, tans elk hides, blacksmiths, and turns out beautiful hand-crafted flintlock rifles. When Buckskin Bill first moved to the Salmon during the Depression years, he was able to live on fifty dollars

60

a year. His garden, wild plants, fish, and game provided food; he made clothing from hides, and tools and utensils from bone and scrap metal left by earlier miners.

Floating the Salmon today, signs of the early settlers are scattered and silent — a few windowless cabins, solitary stone chimneys, and abandoned orchards. It is once more wild country, a domain of elk and eagle, towering cliffs and plunging rapids. The gray-green waters spin through their exquisite corridor of rocks, always moving with a steady, powerful current. As on all whitewater rivers, the challenge of any given rapids depends upon water level. In low water, Salmon Falls is dangerous: the river abruptly drops several vertical feet between huge boulders. In high water, Salmon Falls is barely noticeable. Big Mallard Rapids, rough in any water level, was once inadvertently run after dark by pioneer riverman Harry Guleke. He had beached above the rapids and his party decided to sleep aboard. In the middle of the night a beaver (or beavers) gnawed through both tie ropes, causing the wooden sweepboat to plummet through the crashing water and dark rocks. Miraculously, the boat emerged not only upright but with everyone still aboard.

On the river, one rarely floats for more than a mile or two without passing the mouth of a creek. Adjacent to many of them are low, level benches which make ideal campsites. Bluebells, forget-me-nots, purple and white lupine, and scarlet gilia accent the yellow of grasses, and under the trees are mosses and mushrooms — as well as poison ivy.

A short hike up a side creek will bring you to fishing pools, possibly beaver ponds or cataracts. At dusk, if you walk cautiously, you may encounter a deer momentarily frozen in the shadows beneath the trees even as it tenses to bound away, or a flock of Bighorn sheep watering at the river, ewes wading in first as the rams stand guard. Long after dark, with campfire collapsed into caves of glowing coals and the river sounding its ageless music, it is good to know that places like the Salmon River Canyon have been set aside for everyone, and that those who come to it cannot claim or fence the land, but, like nomads, must pass through and enjoy its beauty.

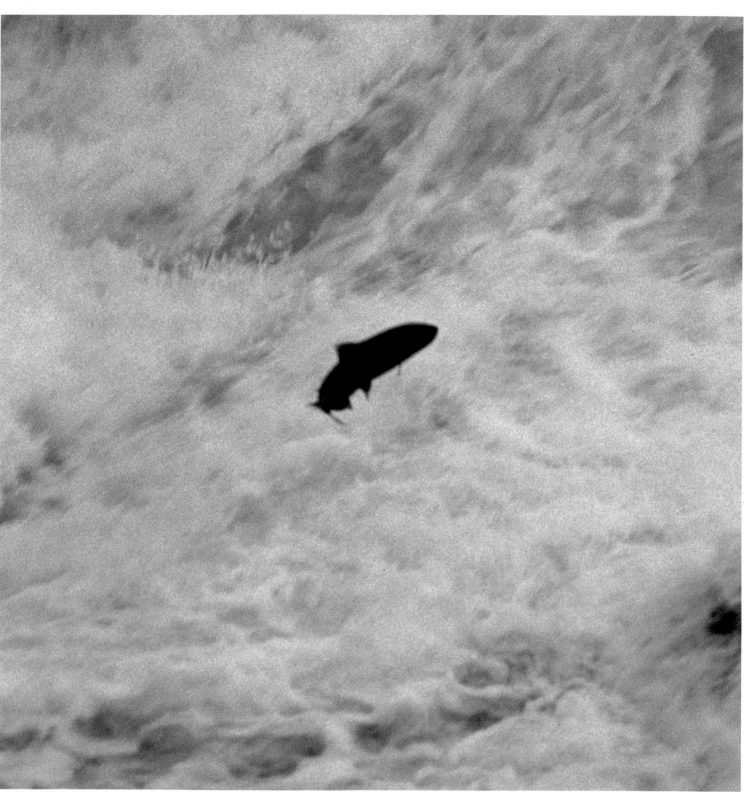

61

Leaping high above a churn of whitewater at the base of Dagger Falls, a salmon fights its way up the wild Middle Fork of the Salmon River to its spawning grounds. Not only is the river famous for its summer salmon runs, but the Middle Fork has long been renowned for trout fishing.

Veil Falls (left) on the Middle Fork of the Salmon River. The rugged canyon of the Middle Fork contains several waterfalls and hot springs. After leading troops down a tributary of the Middle Fork in pursuit of Sheepeater Indians in 1879, U.S. Army Captain Ruben Barnard wrote that "within a distance of ten miles we have come from ten feet of snow to roses and wildflowers."

63

Above, some eighteen miles from its confluence with the Salmon River, the Middle Fork cuts through Impassable Canyon, where granite walls soar from 2,000 to 3,000 feet above the water and boulders rip the current into several violent rapids. For thirty years Earl Parrot, a hermit, lived in a cabin on a ledge above Impassable Canyon.

A dead limber pine (above) stretches gnarled limbs above Sawtooth Lake, one of the headwaters of the Salmon River. Wind-twisted limber pines, which may live for more than two hundred years, are often found at timberline.

Thrusting to an elevation of 11,870 feet above sea level, Castle Peak (top) is the highest point in the White Cloud Mountains. In the spring, melting snows upon its flanks give rise to the East Fork of the Salmon River.

Above, a placid, high-country brook reflects a haunting image of Castle Peak. Prospectors prowled this region in the 1860's and 70's, but today's visitors carry trail guides, climbing equipment, and binoculars rather than picks, shovels, and gold-pans.

65

*Above, snow-draped
peaks of the Sawtooth
Range are reflected on the
surface of Alice Lake,
whose granite bed was
gouged out by glaciers.
The chill body of water
drains into the Upper
Salmon River.*

Alarmed, a Western Diamondback rattlesnake (above left) coils as if to strike on a rocky bank of the Salmon River. Although rattlesnakes will strike people if startled or provoked, their aggressiveness is highly exaggerated; they usually flee or freeze at the approach of man.

At right, the Salmon River slips beneath a weathered granite face near the mouth of Cub Creek. Rocky Mountain sheep, found throughout the Salmon River Canyon, casually leap from ledge to ledge on such precipitous cliffs.

Pictographs (below left) decorate a slab of rock close to the mouth of Stub Creek. Although Indians have lived in the Salmon River Canyon for at least 8,000 years, horses were unknown until introduced by Spanish exploration in the southwest, probably dating this rock art at 1750 or later.

66

Lively Bargamin Creek (left), known as the "Little Salmon" in the early days. In 1920 the creek was renamed for a home-steader who ran a trap line after finding the Colorado Rockies too crowded for his taste.

Bargamin Creek (right) brawls its way down into a quiet stretch of the Salmon River. A hundred million years ago a mass of granite bulged skyward; the Salmon River cut its way through the barrier, and Bargamin Creek, like a number of other tributaries, drops swiftly from wooded highlands several thousand feet above the river.

69

70-71. *The Salmon River swings around an elbow of white sand beach near Paine Creek. Although there are beaches and flats all along this canyon area, it is extremely rugged country. The Lewis and Clark Expedition avoided it, choosing an easier route, and prospectors later nicknamed the Salmon the "River of No Return."*

A bull elk (left), bearing 12-point antlers, wades a tributary of the Salmon River. In autumn, bull elk fight for possession of cows, and an exceptional bull may end up with a harem of sixty or more females. The antlers are shed late in winter.

Dawn mist on the Salmon River, looking downstream from Bull Creek (right). At this time of day, as in the evening, fish jump in eddies and wildlife slips through the forest. The Salmon River country contains deer, black bear, mountain lion, coyote, lynx, a few grizzly bear, and a number of smaller mammals as well as Bighorn sheep and elk.

72

74–75. *The Salmon River (left) sweeps around a bend to merge with the Snake River. Above the confluence, the Snake River twists its way through Hell's Canyon. A depth of 7,900 feet along one stretch makes this the deepest canyon in North America.*

74

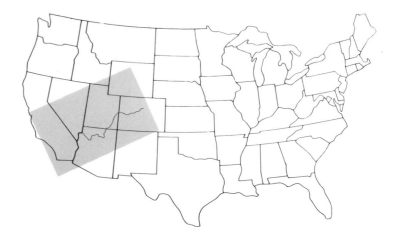

Photographs by David Muench

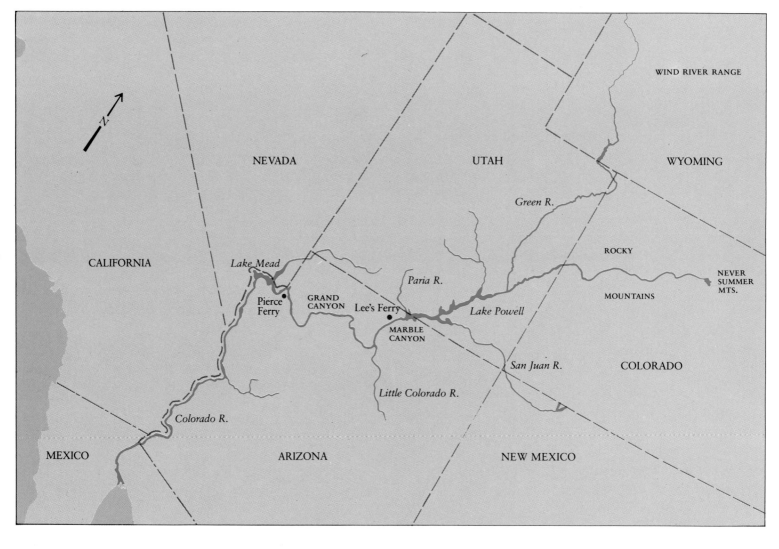

WIND RIVER RANGE

NEVADA   UTAH   WYOMING

Green R.

ROCKY

CALIFORNIA   NEVER
                                                         SUMMER
Lake Mead   MOUNTAINS   MTS.
                        Paria R.
Pierce   GRAND
Ferry   CANYON   Lee's Ferry   Lake Powell
                      MARBLE
                      CANYON
                                          San Juan R.   COLORADO

                      Little Colorado R.

Colorado R.

MEXICO   ARIZONA   NEW MEXICO

0   250 Mi.

0   250 Km.

The Colorado

In 1869 a remarkable naturalist, Major John Wesley Powell, a one-armed veteran of the Civil War, set out to explore the Colorado. Unlike his predecessors, Powell came to the river without visions of what he hoped to find; his calm and patient obsession would be to observe and record what actually was there. The Powell expedition consisted of nine men with four boats. Powell was the only true scientist among them, and none was skilled in river running.

The expedition began at Green River, Wyoming, on the tributary of the same name. The river carried them through the badlands of southwestern Wyoming and Flaming Gorge — now largely buried beneath a reservoir — and into Brown's Hole. Only four decades earlier the latter had been a major rendezvous for fur trappers and Indians. Beyond Brown's Hole the river plunges through the deep and rapids-filled Canyon of Lodore, where Powell lost one of his boats in a rapids that he named Disaster Falls. (In that same treacherous collection of rock and waves the author almost flipped a raft many years later.) Powell pushed on, passing through canyons that had never been explored. His boats then drifted into the junction with the main Colorado and were immediately hurtled through the rapids of Cataract Canyon. Finally they emerged into the quiet waters of Glen Canyon, then an intimate gorge of oak-set glens, fern-hung alcoves, and brilliant rock formations, now lost forever beneath the waters of Lake Powell, in Utah. On August 5 he reached the mouth of the Paria River in Arizona. His diary noted:

With some feeling of anxiety we enter a new canyon this morning. We have learned to observe closely the texture of the rock. In softer strata we have a quiet river, in harder we find rapids and falls. Below us are the limestones and hard sandstones which we found in Cataract Canyon. This bodes toil and danger.

This was prophetic, for in the next 285 miles the river drops 2,000 feet into the depths of the Marble and Grand canyons, thundering over more than 150 rapids. Professional river guides consider this the most challenging navigable stretch of water in the world.

The Colorado begins in the relatively high, cool Never Summer Mountains northwest of Denver and the Wind River Range of Wyoming; it ends in a delta which fans out from the Sonora Desert of Mexico, where the highest temperature on the continent has been recorded. Between the alpine meadows of its origins and the scorched sand, hardpan, and scrub of its delta, the Colorado and its major tributaries have carved their way through hundreds of miles of canyons.

The multihued and layered walls of those canyons depict two billion years of the earth's history, eroded at the rate of less than an inch in ten centuries. The waters of the Colorado have rasped their way down into the vast, dry plateau and together with the wind have bared the rock and shaped it into a monumental yet delicate scrimshaw of arches, bridges, pillars, and pinnacles of every imaginable shape and color.

Man has customarily used great rivers as highways for his commerce; major inland cities are almost invariably situated at promising locations along them. The Colorado defies all this. Only a few towns are scattered along the 1,700-mile length of the river, and for long stretches there are no settlements at all. No roads or railroads flank the river for any appreciable length — serpentine gorges with sheer walls and innumerable rapids quickly discouraged early-day engineers and riverboat operators. As early as 1540, Spaniards had come to the Colorado seeking legendary cities of gold and "pagan" souls ripe for conversion. What they found was a region largely devoid of villages or heathens, yet the stone ruins of a vanished people were everywhere. Later, gold seekers worked their way down from the high-country camps of Colorado, panning and even dredging along the river. They had little better luck than the Spaniards.

For eighty years after Powell's epic voyage, men and women would attempt to run the river, drawn by its promise of adventure and its beauty. Some drowned, but others managed to get through, utilizing a variety of craft. By the mid 1950s, fewer than 150 people had ever gone down the canyons. However, more recently a new kind of expedition has appeared on the river — river guides operating rubber rafts filled with paying passengers. By 1966, one thousand people a year were passing through the canyon, and that number has now increased severalfold, paradoxically overcrowding a wilderness. The National Park Service has put a ceiling on the number of permits they will issue for boat travel in the canyon. Lee's Ferry, a settlement at the mouth of the Paria River, is the embarkation point, or "put-in," for most expeditions running the Marble and Grand canyons today.

Four miles below Lee's Ferry, the Colorado passes beneath the steel arch of Navajo Bridge, which soars 467 feet above the river. Canyon walls polished by wind and weather begin to appear on either side of the calm, green current. This is the Kaibab limestone formation, deposited around 200 million years ago. Fossils of shellfish, corals, and snails indicate that what is now the Kaibab Plateau was then a shallow tropical

sea. As one drifts downriver through Marble Canyon, ever older rock layers appear at water level; these graphically reveal the climate and life of the region all the way back to a time when there was apparently no life at all. At water level, the Kaibab limestone soon gives way to the Toroweap Formation and the Coconino Sandstone, compressed sand dunes of a vast desert over which lizardlike creatures once moved. Although no other trace of these animals has ever been found, the rock has perfectly preserved their tracks as well as the imprints of raindrops which fell millions of years ago.

Thus, observed in just a few days or even a few hours, we come upon clues locked into the rock that take us ever backward in time. Below the yellow Coconino Sandstone is the reddish Hermit Shale, which tells us of the fern-lined rivers and mudflats that preceded the desert. In that time there were insects and ponderous amphibians which probably resembled huge salamanders. Then, beneath the Hermit Shale lies the even more ancient Redwall Limestone, largely deposited in a quiet sea. The life revealed in each successive layer becomes ever more primitive: some of the earliest fish, then sea worms and the armored trilobite, and finally no sign of animal life at all — only algal deposits of microscopic plants. In the depths of Granite Gorge in the Grand Canyon one passes a section of Vishnu Schist some two billion years old and without any signs of life at all.

Badger Creek Rapid, some eight miles below Lee's Ferry, is the first of the many rapids in the canyons. Boatmen rate rapids on a scale of difficulty from one to ten. "One" is a gentle riffle; "ten" is a thundering giant which buries even the largest boat in waves and spray. Badger Creek Rapid is rated "four" to "six," a formidable churn of water which can be tricky depending on the water level. When I ran Marble Canyon, the water level was such that some companions and I floated through Badger Creek Rapids in our life jackets.

Yet there is a great deal more to Marble Canyon than whitewater. Massive rock walls have been shaped and scooped by the river and its tributaries. There is Ten Mile Rock, a vertical slab thrusting up from the green current; Redwall Cavern, a deeply gouged amphitheater which Major Powell reckoned could hold an audience of 50,000 people (who if seated would have to be very, very tightly crowded together, judging from the look of it today, after a century of silting); the deep cleft of Buck Farm Canyon, where the walls close in so narrowly that in places one can touch both walls with outspread arms.

The limestone walls of Marble Canyon are high, magnificent — and arid. When Powell reached a point thirty-two miles downstream from Lee's Ferry, however, he came upon a remarkable sight.

The river turns sharply to the east and seems enclosed by a wall set with a million gems. On coming nearer we find fountains bursting from the rock high overhead, and spray in the sunshine forms the ferns which bedeck the wall. The rocks are covered with mosses and ferns and many beautiful flowering plants. We name it Vasey's Paradise, in honor of the botanist who traveled with us last year.

The confluence of the Colorado with the Little Colorado marks the end of Marble Canyon and the beginning of Grand Canyon. Although the river now swings to the west, there is no break in the canyon walls; geographically, Marble Canyon is, in effect, the upper end of the Grand Canyon. The Little Colorado enters the Grand Canyon out of a profound gorge, a turquoise, mineral-laden current which flows over reefs of deposited minerals. Powell records killing three rattlesnakes there. When I camped there, I was disappointed to have found no snakes at all, as they are among the most interesting and beautiful of desert creatures.

At the mouth of the Little Colorado things have not changed since Powell's time: the terraced walls rising thousands of feet to distant and forested promontories, the clear song of canyon wrens, the alcoves where water seeps and where ferns as well as scarlet monkey flowers grow thickly — and the rapids. We soon began to plunge through some of the truly big drops, rated class six or higher — Hance, Sockdolager, Grapevine, Horn Creek, Granite, and Hermit. In these places the sounds are perhaps even more awesome than the sight of the mad avalanches of water.

Most of the rapids in Grand Canyon were created as a result of summer cloudbursts that sent flash floods racing down side canyons, which are parched for most of the year. When huge boulders are dislodged and pushed down the creekbeds into the river, they obstruct its current, thereby creating rapids. Crystal Rapid, eleven miles beyond where a footbridge links Phantom Ranch with the trail to the south rim of Grand Canyon, was a modest stretch of whitewater until 1966. The day after an unusually violent storm boatmen rounded a bend above Crystal Creek to find the river boiling up into a mass of giant waves. Overnight the great rocks that had been swept down by the creek had turned Crystal into one of the two most challenging rapids on the river, a boat-destroyer of awesome power.

The river continues to slice ever deeper into the rock. Powell wrote on August 14, 1869: "The gorge is black and narrow below, red and gray and flaring above with crags and angular projections on the walls. Down in these grand gloomy depths we glide, ever listening, ever watching."

It is as if the river were trying to carve its way into the very marrow of the earth. Granite Gorge exposes a section of Vishnu Schist, as old a rock as man has yet seen. The black and dark green cliff is carved and polished as if it were a single, massive piece of sculpture. Here in the gorge, cliffs of hard schists, granites, and pegmatite rise steeply from the water. Sand, blown from terraces high above, has drifted against the rock walls. In the summer, heat radiates off the rock, turning the gorge into an inferno where the temperature can climb to 120 degrees in the shade by mid-afternoon. The same place may be brutally cold in the winter. Yet for all of the temperature extremes, a variety of hardy plants thrives here. We found cactus — cholla, prickly pear, fish-hook — seemingly growing out of the very rock in talus slopes and on high cliff crannies. There is much brittlebrush, tea, and catclaw.

One of the magical elements of the Grand Canyon is its side streams and washes. The contrast between a place like Elves Chasm, with its clear pools and a delicate verdancy of mosses and ferns, and the raw, monumental rock forms of the canyon is extravagant. 79

Thunder River is actually a gigantic spring which bursts from a high canyon wall and tumbles down through thickets of willow, hackberry, box elder, and cottonwood into the crystalline, chilly waters of Tapeats Creek, which itself reaches the river through an exuberant series of cascades and drops. One of the more beautiful walks to be found anywhere is the trail that takes one up Tapeats Creek, through Surprise Valley, and then back to the river beside Deer Creek. Deer Creek plunges into the river as a waterfall which has all but turned to fine mist before striking rock at its base.

Some twenty miles downriver from Deer Creek the turquoise waters of Havasu Creek enter the Colorado from the south. Here, too, the colors of the canyon are incredibly varied — the red limestone, the unusual blue of the creek which is mostly caused by suspended clay particles, the vivid greens of grasses, the cottonwoods, wild celery, and subtle shades of orchids. Havasu Creek approaches the Colorado over a series of spectacular waterfalls. At Bridal Veil the water, falling from a height of 170 feet, is actually a series of individual streams which break into plumes of mist upon ledges below. The isolated village of Supai, eight miles up from the Colorado at the extreme western end of the canyon, is home to about two hundred members of the Havasupai tribe, who cultivate orchards of apricots, figs, and peaches, as well as fields of alfalfa, corn, beans, squash, and melons. The Havasupais have an unhurried way of life, living close to the earth. Powell's journal entry for August 25 read:

Great quantities of lava are seen on either side; and then we come to an abrupt cataract. Just over the fall a cinder cone, or extinct volcano, stands on the very brink of the canyon. What a conflict of water and fire there must have been here!

Remnants of that ancient fiery flow, which once completely barricaded the canyon, today rip the river's current into foam and spray. This is Lava Falls, perhaps the most difficult rapids in the world that is run with any regularity. The river abruptly drops thirty-seven feet, crashing through a joyous nightmare of basalt boulders and gigantic holes, some of which may heave the onrushing water into a standing wave twenty feet high or more, depending on the water level. Lava Falls arouses within even the most experienced riverman excitement, respect, and perhaps something of what a matador might experience if he had to take on two dangerous bulls simultaneously.

The river, still walled by towering layers of rock which embody a mute saga of long-vanished seas and extinct creatures, continues to wind toward the Gulf of California. As in all desert country, it is the contrasts which astonish and delight. Here the river takes a bend to afford a breathtaking panorama of monumental proportions. Then the river narrows, providing a close view of rock that has been carved into unique forms by the river's sand over the centuries. There are small bone-white sand beaches where the only signs of life may be a single mustard plant and the tracks of a lizard. Yet on other beaches there is a profusion of desert plants as well as birds and small animals. Bighorn sheep pick their way along the crags, and a sizable population of burros, descendants of the pack animals that strayed from early-day prospectors, can be found in the lower canyon. Finally, there is the juxtaposition of clear, cold water within side canyons and the scorched and naked rock.

Powell's voyage of exploration ended at Grand Wash Cliffs in Arizona, close to modern day Lake Mead, exactly a hundred days after his party left Green River, Wyoming. Although two members of his expedition continued on to tidewater, Powell himself headed back to civilization. His goal was exploration and scientific observation; the lower river had already been traced by the expedition of Lieutenant Joseph Ives about a decade earlier. After his return to civilization, Powell wrote:

You cannot see the Grand Canyon in one view, as if it were a changeless spectacle from which a curtain might be lifted, but to see it you have to toil from month to month through its labyrinths. It is a region more difficult to traverse than the Alps or the Himalayas, but if strength and courage are sufficient for the task, by a year's toil a concept of sublimity can be obtained never again to be equaled on the higher side of Paradise.

81

Kawuneeche Valley, Rocky Mountain National Park (above). Here, close to the headwaters of the Colorado River, streams are checked by a series of beaver dams. Although the Colorado River itself begins in Rocky Mountain National Park, the tributary Green River, which rises in the Wind River Mountains of Wyoming, is longer.

82–83. Sunrise at Dead Horse Point State Park, Utah. A gnarled juniper overlooks the Colorado River, looping through layers of ancient rock two thousand feet below. A dirt road (foreground) follows the contour of the White Rim, a layer of hard sandstone which is sandwiched between softer formations of dark red siltstone.

Above left, beneath the rim of Grand View Point, Canyonlands National Park, spires and isolated walls rise from the shaded depths of Monument Canyon. From Grand View Point, the tip of a plateau wedged between deeply incised canyons of the Colorado and Green Rivers, wondrous contortions of bare and intricately carved rock sprawl in three directions.

Plantlike clusters of ice (below left) floating down the Colorado River provide haunting contrasts to mirrorlike canyon walls. Spring floods of the Colorado, swollen with snowmelt from the western slope of the Rocky Mountains, have carved awesome canyons whose rock layers depict two billion years of geologic history.

At right, a well-preserved tower of tightly fitted stone looms above a sandstone cliff in Horse Canyon, Canyonlands National Park. Built by Indians of the Fremont Culture 700 to 1,000 years ago, this structure may have been a ceremonial site, a watchtower, or a storage bin.

Early-morning dust storm at Gunsight Arm, Lake Powell (left). For much of its 1,700-mile length, the Colorado River and its canyons resemble the landscapes nineteenth-century illustrators attributed to the surfaces of distant planets.

At right, late afternoon sun creates another sort of magic upon Lake Powell, where fingers of blue water reach deep into walls of vivid sandstone. Created by back-up from Glen Canyon Dam, the lake inundated Glen Canyon, which was one of the most beautiful stretches of the entire Colorado.

87

88–89. *A low autumn sun highlights a row of steep, multicolored buttes lining the southeastern rim of Lake Powell and accents the rich blue of this deep reservoir. The edge of Navajo Mountain, a huge volcanic swell which is sacred to the Navajo Tribe, rises in the distance at the upper left.*

Rainbow Bridge vaults
309 feet near Aztec Creek,
which flows into Lake
Powell. The magnificent
arch is today only a short
hike upstream from a
marina on Lake Powell.
When the author first
visited the bridge before
the filling of the lake, he
had to use a sixteen-mile
trail which descended
deeply cut canyons next to
Navajo Mountain.

After John and Louisa
Wetherill established a
trading post at Oljato,
Utah, in 1906, Indians
told them of a great arch
off in the slick rock
country to the west. It
was not until 1909 that
the first party of white
men viewed the span.
English author J. B.
Priestley would later
write: "How do we know
that Rainbow Bridge is

not itself a kind of
symphony, no more to be
completely explained by
geology than Beethoven is
by acoustics?"

92–93. *At sunset, the upper cliffs of Marble Canyon gleam like layers of solid gold. A band of Spanish soldiers reached the rim of Grand Canyon, immediately south of Marble Canyon, in 1540, seeking legendary cities of gold. Finding no precious metals, they withdrew, and these deeply slashed canyons were all but forgotten until the expedition led by John Wesley Powell more than three centuries later.*

93

94–95. *From Lipan Point, on the south rim of the Grand Canyon, slashed side gorges fall away to the Colorado River below. Here Major Powell wrote: "We are three-quarters of a mile in the depths of the earth and the great river shrinks into insignificance as it dashes its angry waves against the walls and cliffs that rise to the world above."*

94

96

Above, four views of the Grand Canyon from Point Imperial on the North Rim. Both the scope and subtleties of the Grand Canyon are staggering, as the nuances of dawn (far left), midday (center left) and sunset (right) suggest. Mt. Hayden is the prominent peak in the distance.

98–99. *As seen from Desert Tower, on the South Rim, a thunderstorm sweeps across distant rock terraces of the Grand Canyon. Few places upon the planet exhibit such dramatic shifts of weather, for, as one shelf of rock is pounded by a downpour or a hailstorm, a clump of twisted junipers a mile away will be in sunlight.*

Royal Arch Creek (left) sprays into a clear pool at Elves Chasm, one of several water-sculpted alcoves which open into the Colorado River in the depths of Grand Canyon. Mosses and ferns spring from narrow ledges and cracks in the rock.

Detail of Deer Creek Falls (right). The falls delighted Powell in 1869, causing him to write: "Just after dinner we pass a stream on the right, which leaps into the Colorado by a direct fall of more than 100 feet, forming a beautiful cascade. On the rocks in the cavelike chamber are ferns, with delicate fronds and enameled stalks."

102–103. *The Colorado glides through the stark magnificence of its inner gorge just above Havasu Canyon. Although the Powell expedition was the first party to intentionally voyage Grand Canyon, an itinerant trapper named James White may have rafted through the canyon two years before.*

104–105. *Distorted by atmosphere, a seemingly enormous sun washes ragged thrusts of rock at the western end of Grand Canyon with a vivid outpouring of colors. It is on the Colorado, perhaps more than any other place upon the Earth, that one has a sense of being close to the ancient, powerful forces of creation.*

106–107. *Greggs Hideout, Lake Mead. Emerging from the lofty stone corridors of Grand Canyon, the Colorado flows into Lake Mead, which was created by Hoover Dam and is rimmed by dry, eroded desert ranges. Some of the caves in the area are filled with bat guano; others contain remains of the extinct giant ground sloth.*

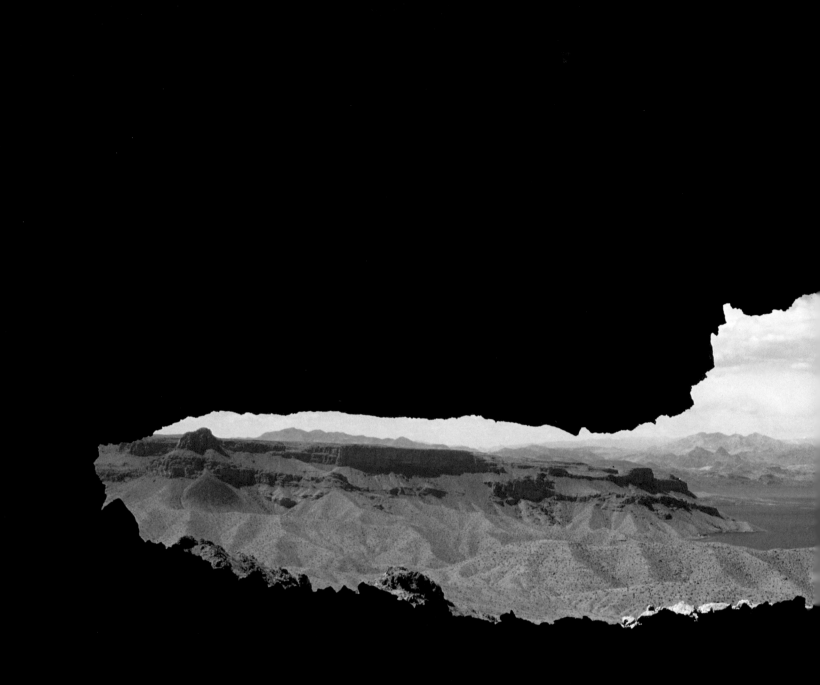

106

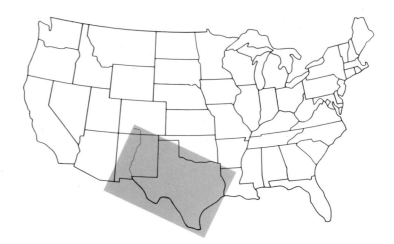

Photographs by David Muench

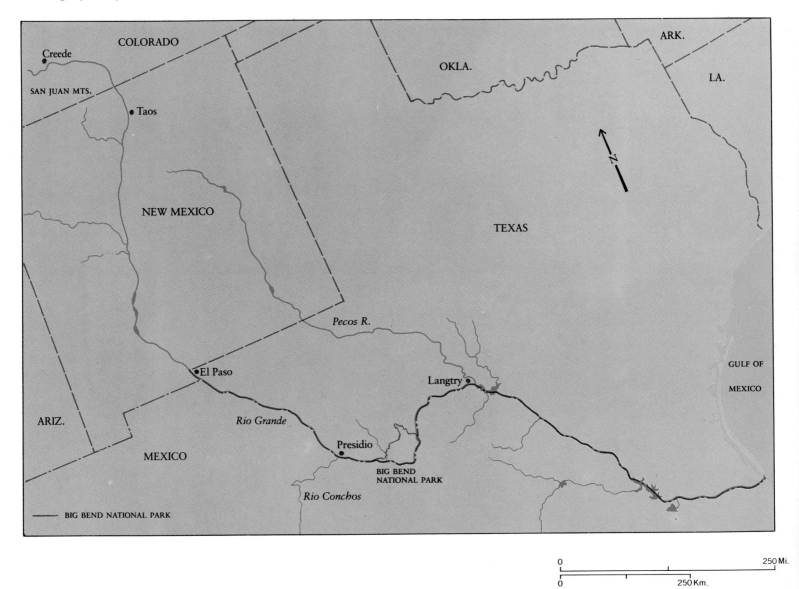

COLORADO

Creede

SAN JUAN MTS.

Taos

NEW MEXICO

ARIZ.

MEXICO

Rio Grande

Presidio

Rio Conchos

El Paso

Pecos R.

OKLA.

ARK.

LA.

N

TEXAS

Langtry

BIG BEND
NATIONAL PARK

GULF OF

MEXICO

—— BIG BEND NATIONAL PARK

0   250 Mi.

0   250 Km.

The Rio Grande

Beartown, Colorado consists of an old stagecoach station with a roof crushed by the weight of winter snows, the scattered debris of a mining mill, and an abandoned cabin in a large meadow. During the late summer and early autumn the lush grass of the clearing is scattered with the bright reds of Indian paintbrush, and the subtler tones of the yellow arnica and white globeflower. Elk feed in this meadow at times, and so do flocks of sheep. The sheep are herded by Basques who have often recently arrived from Spain and know little or no English. Beartown is close to the timberline; towering peaks — some of them over 14,000 feet high — loom to the west, north, and south. Only to the east does the land fall precipitously away to canyons and valleys thousands of feet below.

Stony Pass (elevation 12,588 ft.) notches a serrated ridge to the west of Beartown. Here, in late spring, trickles of melting snow become rivulets which merge into engorged creeks and pummel their way downward between strands of Engelmann spruce, Subalpine fir, and aspens. Once united, they form a young, rambunctious river which plunges through a deep and narrow gorge and meanders down grassy mountain valleys.

Thus begins the Rio Grande, which soon swings south out of Colorado to flow the length of New Mexico before becoming the border between Texas and Mexico. As such, it finally spreads into salt marshes on the Gulf of Mexico, 1,885 miles from its source above Beartown. It is the second longest river in the contiguous United States — only the Missouri-Mississippi system covers more territory. As rivers go, it is not large, having few tributaries. For most of its length it passes over dry plains or through arid canyons; cottonwood trees, tamarisk, and other bankside growth draw off a large amount of water and most of the spring runoff is diverted for irrigation. On occasion, the river completely dries up in the desert below El Paso, Texas.

The Rio Grande may not be a large river but it cuts its way through some of the most spectacular wild country in America. The Rio Grande Gorge of northern New Mexico was one of the initial components of the National Wild and Scenic Rivers System. For 250 miles, between Big Bend National Park and Langtry, Texas, the river pushes its way through canyons which have been deeply incised into gaunt desert ranges.

In 1536, four ragged and starving men stumbled into an Indian village close to the present site of El Paso. Alvar Nunez Cabeza de Vaca and his three companions were the sole survivors of a Spanish expedition which had landed in Florida eight years before. After living among southeastern Indian tribes, first as slaves and later as medicine men, they finally began an epic westward journey, hoping to reach Spanish settlements on the Pacific coast. They were the first Europeans to see the Rio Grande. Four years after they reached the safety of a Spanish outpost, an army led by Francisco Vasquez de Coronado arrived at the banks of the Rio

Grande near present day Albuquerque, seeking the legendary cities of Cibola, where rooftops were said to be tiled with gold and entire streets were lined with the shops of silversmiths.

Although Coronado and his fellow *conquistadores* probed westward until they came to the rim of the Grand Canyon, they found no golden cities — and not even any precious metals. More than three centuries later, however, silver was discovered in the San Juan Mountains, which cup the headwaters of the Rio Grande. By 1873 prospectors were swarming into the region. The first big strikes were made on the Animas River, on the other side of Stony Pass, and most of the early arrivals hurried up the Rio Grande to its headwaters without pausing to prospect along the way. Then, in 1889, the excitement shifted to Willow Creek, a tributary of the Rio Grande, with the opening of the Holy Moses Mine. Creede, a boom town of tents and false-front buildings, soon lined Willow Creek and began to spill onto the flats below.

Today, Creede is a quiet village. Four-wheel drive vehicles have replaced the stagecoaches which used to jounce along the wagon road to the headwaters of the Rio Grande at Stony Pass. Bald eagles, hunted to the brink of extinction during the silver boom, have made a dramatic comeback. So have elk. During the summer months, an estimated 10,000 elk browse the high meadows of the upper Rio Grande drainage. Not infrequently, herds are seen above timberline, feeding upon tundra mosses.

Below Creede, the river loops through lush meadowlands and thick strands of cottonwood before entering a steep-sided canyon near Wagon Wheel Gap. This canyon, with its fast, clear water, is the site of an annual summer raft race. The Rio Grande emerges from the mountains to flow across the San Luis Valley, a wide flat prairie which is 8,000 feet above sea level, and noted for the chill of its winters. To the northeast, gigantic sand dunes are piled at the base of ragged peaks bearing perpetual snow. The current is leisurely here. Frame farmhouses sit back from the river. Near the New Mexican border, the river begins to drop below the horizon line of the prairie and the current quickens. This is the beginning of the Rio Grande Gorge, where the river cuts its way down into

the lava flows of ancient volcanos, a fifty-mile chasm that is so abrupt that a man can ride horseback to within fifty yards of it in most places without realizing it is there. The gorge is 800 feet deep along one section.

The Rio Grande has many moods within the gorge. In places it swirls gently past banks lined with tamarisk and willow. Raccoons and skunks slip quietly through the undergrowth and mule deer drink at the water's edge at dawn and twilight. Elsewhere, the drop exceeds 100 feet to the mile, and the river thunders and spurts its way through house-high boulders — areas that defy passage to even the most accomplished river runners. Close to the confluence of Red River, Big Arsenic Springs pushes out 5,400 gallons of pure, cold water every minute. In deep, eddying pools nearby, large brown and rainbow trout fatten on crayfish. Anglers have taken ten-pound trout there. Hawks and occasional golden eagles glide on thermal currents between lichen-stained walls.

When these raptors spot prey upon ledges or in the jumble of boulders at the edge of the river, they fold their wings and plunge downward, talons spread to snatch off their victims — desert rats and other rodents, lizards, and snakes. Rattlesnakes, king snakes, and bull snakes are common in the gorge, but are rarely seen. Rattlers are so affected by the extremes of heat and cold which prevail in this deep, narrow trench that they spend an average of seventeen out of twenty-four hours in their burrows or beneath rocks. Their reptilian cousins, the lizards, are far more visible, making short, erratic rushes across rock faces or pausing to peer about while rearing up on their crooked front legs. There are all manner of lizards here: the blue-tailed, three-toed, horned, collared, spotted, and banded. Only the iguana seems to be absent.

At first glance, this gut of seared lava would seem inhospitable to plant life. Yet pushing up from narrow benches of soil and from black sand between boulders are several hundred species, most of them small, hardy, and subtle. Along with a variety of cactus, whose blossoms are strikingly vivid against the dark rock, there are wild grasses, yucca, and agave. Evergreen — cedar, pinyon, and juniper — are found in side canyons and provide cover above the rims.

The least accessible section of the gorge stretches south from below the mouth of the Rio Hondo to the Rio Grande's confluence with the Taos River. Trails become increasingly faint and even disappear where great slabs of cliff have fallen from the almost vertical walls. Early Spanish settlers called this the Rio Bravo — Wild River. During the high water of the spring runoff, boatmen in rafts and kayaks thread their way between boulders and swoop down through rapids. None of the individual rapids approaches the size of those in Grand Canyon, yet they expose closely spaced rocks at many water levels. A person caught in one rapids may be washed through two others before he can struggle ashore. A veteran river guide, who rafted this section on the crest of a record runoff, called it "the toughest eighteen miles in America."

Every rapids has its own voice. Approaching Powerline Rapids, a deep, steady roar leaves little doubt that this is a big one — a place where the river devours boats. A rockslide has squeezed the current into an awesome, thundering cascade. Even highly skilled boatmen feel an edge of fear as they approach the smooth tongue of such a drop, and then the sheer exhilaration once they experience the rush of whitewater chaos. Even though boulders, deep holes, and massive standing waves can and often do buckle or flip rafts, for a few moments the riders are as one with the force of the river itself. Beyond Powerline Rapids, submerged boulders and horns of rock thrusting out of water tear the current into five miles of almost continuous rapids. Attempts to bail the water out of a raft between rapids is a labor of Sisyphus; another big wave will soon fill it. Madness. Wonderful madness. Else why do otherwise rational people come back to the most violent rivers year after year?

Below the joining of the Rio Grande and the Taos River, the slab-sided gorge opens into a broader canyon, where there is room enough for a road beside the river and occasional flats containing adobe ranch houses, apple orchards, and fields of chili peppers. White Rock Canyon, some fifty miles to the south, is the final wilderness stretch of the upper river. The current, over the ages, has sliced its way into layers of basalt and tuff — compressed volcanic ash. Several narrow-sided canyons enter from the west, where the ruins of numerous Pueblo Indian villages sprawl across mesa tops or hug vertical rock walls. Each of these high-walled canyons is unique. In one canyon, Frijoles Creek, which has a perennial flow, plunges over two graceful waterfalls close to the Rio Grande; the creek in Capulin Canyon sinks into sand a couple of miles before reaching the river. Lower Alamo Canyon carries water only in time of flood, although the wind rushing through supple ponderosa pines often sounds like a large and lively stream. There are hoodoos here, great conical stones eroded into weird and wonderful shapes, which seem almost to be alive. Camped beneath them on a moonless night, one wonders if they do actually move. All of the canyons contain Indian rock art, but the most spectacular are at Painted Cave in Capulin Canyon, where a long panel depicting animals, masked dancers, the mythical plumed serpent, sun, cloud, and other symbols is dominated by a monstrous snarling red beast.

Beyond Cochiti Lake at the mouth of White Rock Canyon, the river winds its way leisurely down the length of the state. Its waters irrigate the farms which border the river for much of its passage through New Mexico, the flow dwindling with each league to the south. The dry lands of sand and stone, cactus and creosote, press at the perimeters of these green strips, usually no more than a mile or two from the banks. There is a paradox in this aridity, for there are wooded mountains within a day's walk from almost any point on this stretch of the river. The clear, spring-fed streams they contain sink into sands long before reaching the Rio Grande. The only dependable tributaries — the Conejos, Hondo, Taos, Red, and Chama rivers — are on the upper reaches of the Rio Grande. Elsewhere the numerous arroyos feeding into the river are dry except during brief and violent summer thunderstorms, when roiling muddy water rages bank to bank down these watercourses.

At Ojinaga, the Rio Conchos of Mexico adds its flow to that of the depleted Rio Grande. The river moves briskly through a series of short redrock canyons. A road more or less follows the river to Lajitas, a general store where huge catfish heads dangle from the limbs of a cottonwood. Here the river veers away from the road and heads directly for the 3,884-foot-high limestone bulk of Mesa de Anguilla. Until you almost reach the rim of the mesa it seems as if the river must either skirt it or reach a dead end, as there is no sign of a canyon entrance. Then, at the last minute, you notice a deep, vertical cleft, and the current carries your boat into the heart of the rock itself. Thus one enters Santa Elena Canyon at the edge of Big Bend National Park. Although the current is strong and crossrips can abruptly turn a raft or canoe completely around, the only rapids is less than a mile from the entrance of the canyon. At the Rockslide, as it is aptly named, huge water-polished boulders break the river into a maze of dangerous suckholes, undercut ledges, sudden drops, and blind alleys.

About three-fourths of the way through Santa Elena Canyon, a small spring-fed stream tumbles into the Rio Grande after dropping over a series of falls and cascades. Tapestries of fern and other moisture-loving plants hang from the rocks. Frogs and salamanders inhabit long, narrow pools which space out the fast water. Water-striders sprint across the surface of the river.

The exit from Santa Elena Canyon is as abrupt as its entrance. The river spreads out and the current slows, washing willow-bordered banks. The bird Mexicans call brasita de fuega ("little coal of fire") darts back and forth in the foliage, black wings fanning against a red body. To the east, the blue and wooded slopes of the Chisos Mountains lift against the horizon, forcing the Rio Grande into the distinctive elbow known as the Big Bend. Mariscal Canyon is at the southernmost tip of this long crook. Like Santa Elena Canyon, it begins without preamble. The river suddenly slips into a narrow crack in the towering limestone. In places, cliffs rise 1,800 feet above the water.

Midway through the canyon, the walls are bisected by a fault rift known as The Break. An ancient trail fords the river here, passing up the dry washes on either side of border before splitting into numerous, fainter paths. No one can say which Indians first walked this route, but it is known that Comanches rode it to plunder Mexican ranchitos for horses and other livestock. Renegade sheriffs, Civil War deserters, and "badhats" from the plains of Texas drove their own herds of rustled Mexican ponies up the trail and, in turn, Mexican bandits stormed back up The Break seeking longhorns and Indian babies for the slave trade.

In Big Bend National Park and its immediate vicinity, one occasionally encounters people. Paved roads end at picnic and camping areas at two places on the river. There are three hamlets on the Mexican border. Beyond the Mexican mining village of La Linda, however, one enters one of the loneliest stretches of river in the country. A man could canoe for a week — all the way to Langtry, over 120 miles downriver — without seeing another human being. Spanish explorers once planned to establish a series of forts here, but were soon discouraged by the harshness of the terrain: canyon after canyon slashing through gaunt, dry ranges, flats where dust devils whirled toward mirage. They wrote it off as despoplado — desolate wilderness.

The despoplado begins at Outlaw Flats, over which the flat-topped bulk of El Capitan looms in the distance, rising a sheer 1,000 feet above the desert floor. Nameless ridges lift closer at hand, stippled with yucca, candalilla, ocatillo, and prickly pear. The canyons begin, each unique, yet each also part of a greater whole. As individual names begin to blur into each other, senses sharpen. A pebble dislodged by a distant lizard is heard distinctly. Tracks found in sand on the banks of the river become omens.

The contrast between water, seared rock, and vibrant green is sensual. Rapids split the river into chaos. Wild burros gaze at you with mild curiosity. The muggy smell of plants at the water's edge rises. You may see bands of peccary stamping through canebrakes or stands of salt cedar; you are not likely to see the graceful stalking of a mountain lion, although they are here, up in the rocks, waiting for darkness before they prowl. Sunsets flare over contorted ridges where no man has ever walked, let alone named. The world of automobiles, streetlights, and electrical gadgets seems a thousand miles away. The canyons, the truly wild country, ends at Langtry, a huddle of adobe houses where the legendary Judge Roy Bean once held forth as "the law west of the Pecos."

113

Spring thaw on the South Fork of the Rio Grande River above Del Norte, Colorado. The Rio Grande is the second longest river in the contiguous United States — only the Missouri-Mississippi is longer — yet for most of its length it wanders through desert country with few tributaries, and most of its flow comes from melting Rocky Mountain snowpacks at its headwaters.

114

North Clear Creek Falls,
San Juan Mountains,
southwestern Colorado.
After wandering across a
brushy meadow, this lively
tributary of the upper Rio
Grande abruptly plunges
one hundred feet into a
basalt chasm.

Detail (above), North
Clear Creek Falls. In the
San Juan Mountains,
which cradle the quick,
clear headwater streams of
the Rio Grande, are found
some of the highest peaks
in the United States
outside of Alaska.

At left, the upper Rio Grande, here little more than a stream, cuts at the base of a lichen-stained basalt cliff. Aspens, intermingled with Colorado blue spruce, flaunt their autumn colors. Aspen leaves tend to quiver at the slightest breeze, creating a shimmering effect.

117

Spring runoff, Creede Canyon, San Juan Mountains (above). In 1540 Francisco Vásquez de Coronado led an expedition up the Rio Grande River from the present-day site of El Paso, Texas, to Albuquerque, New Mexico, lured by legends of gold and silver. He found neither, but more than three centuries later, silver strikes at the headwaters of the Rio Grande created a stampede of prospectors into the area.

After leaving the mountains of Colorado (left), the Rio Grande River crosses into New Mexico and enters the Rio Grande Gorge, an abrupt fifty-mile-long chasm which has been cut through layers of volcanic rock. Here, the sheer-sided gorge is 800 feet deep.

At right, the pure, cold waters of Big Arsenic Springs issue from a rockslide in the Rio Grande Gorge. In the spring of 1970 this gorge was the first waterway to be dedicated as part of the National Wild and Scenic Rivers System.

120–121. *A winter storm descends onto Santa Elena Canyon at the western end of Big Bend National Park, Texas. Here the Rio Grande, the border between the United States and Mexico, has cut a precipitous gorge through the limestone bulk of Mesa de Anguilla. The Mexican shore is on the left.*

120

Santa Elena Canyon (left) in January. Between the canyons of northern New Mexico and the desert southwest of El Paso, Texas, the Rio Grande is a placid river flanked by farms. Approaching the Big Bend, however, it begins to slice through a series of mountain barriers.

At right, confluence of the Rio Grande and Terlingua Creek, at the mouth of Santa Elena Canyon. The cobblestones in the foreground may have been deposited by a flash flood of the creek or carried into the Rio Grande by the Rio Conchos, which drains the Sierra Madre Occidental of Mexico.

123

124–125. *Evening shadows the mouth of Santa Elena Canyon. The gorge ends as abruptly as it begins. The forested Chisos Mountains, which the river skirts to the south, rise in the distance.*

Limestone caves (below) frame the entrance of Boquillas Canyon, at the eastern end of Big Bend National Park. Such caves are often used as dens by mountain lions which prowl this region. Between Boquillas Canyon and Langtry, Texas, the river passes through 120 miles of roadless, uninhabited desert canyons and mirage-haunted flats.

126

128–129. Mesquite, ebony, and cottonwood line the Mexican side of the Rio Grande near Falcon, Texas. The rounded foreground rocks are concretions — hard, mineralized rocks which have become bonded within softer sedimentary deposits. With the canyon country far behind it, the Rio Grande now becomes a leisurely flow noted for

its large catfish. Here, ranching predominates, but the river soon enters an irrigated region of truck farms and orchards.

130–131. Waves of the Gulf of Mexico lap a shell-strewn beach at Brazos Island State Park, Texas, which lies at the mouth of the Rio Grande. Between the swift trout streams of its headwaters

and the marshes and broad beaches of its delta, the Rio Grande threads its way across dry plains and through scorched canyons. Its water, whether for irrigation or human uses, is more than coveted — men have killed for it. Spanish explorers called it Rio Bravo, Wild River, and certain stretches are even today well deserving of the name

Photographs by Annie Griffiths

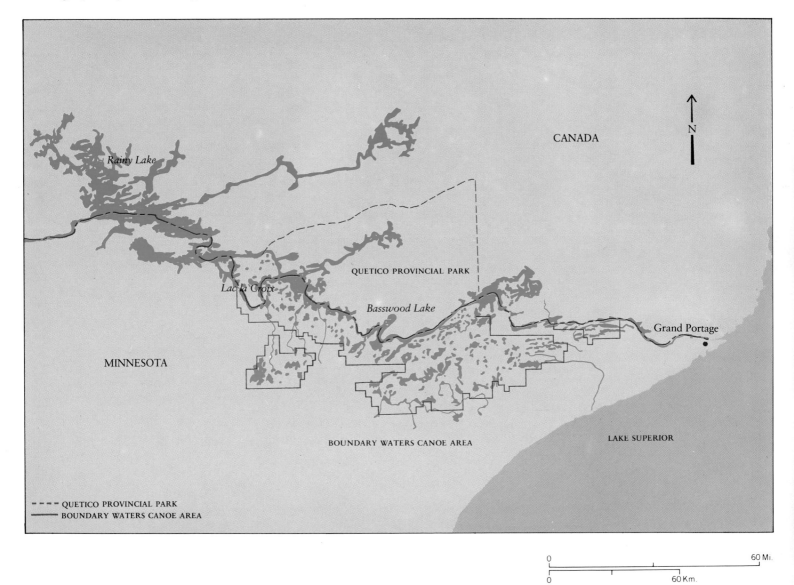

CANADA

N

Rainy Lake

QUETICO PROVINCIAL PARK

Lac la Croix

Basswood Lake

Grand Portage

MINNESOTA

BOUNDARY WATERS CANOE AREA

LAKE SUPERIOR

- - - - QUETICO PROVINCIAL PARK
———— BOUNDARY WATERS CANOE AREA

0   60 Mi.

0   60 Km.

The Boundary Waters

Much of North America was explored to satisfy the quirk of fashion that decreed beaver hats for gentlemen. In the autumn of 1731 the Sieur de la Verendrye led an expedition of French beaver trappers up a steep nine-mile portage at the western end of Lake Superior. Verendrye carried a map which an Indian guide had sketched on a piece of birchbark. From the top of the portage they crossed a chain of lakes to a low divide. Here they paused, and looked out over the waterway that wound off to the west. Would it eventually lead, as Verendrye fervently hoped, to the Pacific Ocean? And how would the trapping be?

As men of action rather than speculation, they soon shoved off, little realizing that they had crossed from the Atlantic watershed to that of Hudson Bay, or that they were entering a beaver trapper's paradise. For hundreds of miles to the north and west the country had been scoured to bedrock by a succession of icecaps in the dim past. After the retreat of the last glacier, thousands of ponds and lakes remained, connected by rivers and streams which contained beaver in undreamed-of numbers.

Using a number of short portages, Verendrye pioneered a route along what is now roughly the Minnesota-Canada border, swung north into the vastness of Lake Winnipeg and eventually reached the upper Missouri River by a portage from the Assiniboine River. The explorer, although frustrated in his hopes of finding a "Northwest Passage" to the Pacific, had opened a great trade route. Canoes bearing cargoes of guns, kettles, axes, beads, cloth, tobacco, and other goods were paddled over a 3,000-mile trunk route which led from Montreal to Fort Chipewyan on Lake Athabaska, and then returned laden with beaver pelts.

The boatmen, called *voyageurs*, were a hardy breed who could paddle eighteen hours a day with only a short break every hour for a pull at their pipes; and they thought nothing of portaging 180-pound loads. Although they passed over waters teeming with fish, they had little time to catch them. The *voyageurs'* basic diet was pemmican — a mixture of fat, dried buffalo meat, and dried berries. There was always time for song, however, and a man with a headful of tunes and lyrics was much esteemed among his fellows.

Even as the fur trade was reaching up into the Arctic where trees had dwindled to dwarfs, and to the chill rivers rushing out of the Rocky Mountains, Americans were moving westward, clearing farms and establishing settlements. As the pace of life to the south of the *voyageur* route quickened, the fur trade began to languish. The supply of readily accessible beaver was depleted and, more importantly, the beaver hat was no longer in demand. By the time cities such as Detroit, Cincinnati, and Chicago were impatiently pushing upward and outward, most of the fur-trading posts had been abandoned, and the North Country was almost as much of a wilderness as when the first *voyageurs* passed through it.

To preserve some of this empire of woods, lakes, and rivers, the U.S. government had designated over one million acres of northern Minnesota as the Boundary Waters Canoe Area, a region without roads, where development is prohibited and powerboats are restricted to a few areas. Even carrying of disposable cans and bottles into the area is prohibited. A similar wilderness expanse, the Quetico Provincial Park, stretches along the Canadian side of the border.

Over a million years ago, what is now a maze of lakes and streams was a hilly country with well-defined watersheds and a cover of hardwood trees. Gradually, the air turned colder and drier; winters lengthened until the accumulated snows were compressed into clear, blue ice which finally moved slowly away from the greatest centers of pressure like a system of bewitched rivers. Ice hundreds of feet thick pushed across most of eastern Canada and south into the Mississippi Valley.

When the icecap retreated for the last time only eleven thousand years ago, the land had been violently altered. Softer hills had been scraped away, more resistant rock knobs polished, and the bedrock gouged with massive furrows. Snowmelt and rainwater filled the innumerable depressions. Over a period of centuries the forces of gravity dictated an immensely complicated pattern of flow toward Hudson Bay. From a map, it is often almost impossible to tell whether a stream is feeding into or out of a lake, or even which way a waterfall is tumbling.

There are over 1,200 miles of canoe trails in the Boundary Waters Canoe Area and Quetico Provincial Park. Although it is accessible from a number of rivers and lakes on either side of the border, the town of Ely, Minnesota, is the most popular gateway.

The early summer is a good time to see wildlife. Migratory birds are returning from warmer climates, including the bobolink, which winters over four thousand miles on the *pampas* of Brazil and Argentina. Black bear, ravenously hungry from their almost foodless winter sleep, prowl the woods in search of ground squirrels, mice, grubs, ants, bird eggs, plant food — such as tubers — and other favorite foods.

Moose chew young leaves with what seems like a dreamy deliberation. By August, the warmest month in the North Country, the insects are largely gone, as is the best fishing. The most popular canoe routes tend to become crowded, although there are still a great many lonely stretches of water.

Early autumn is my favorite season in the Boundary Waters. Chippewa Indians speak of it as the season when gods kill the Great Bear, whose blood and roasted fat drippings stain the leaves. Frequently a period of overcast skies, wind, and monotonous rain is followed by a brief Indian summer, when the sun is soft in a deep blue sky. Breezes ripple through groves of birch and other hardwoods; the portage paths are carpeted with red and yellow leaves. Just before dawn, mist rises from glass-still water, often turning slowly like a mock tornado. At this time of year, storms may sweep over a camp quite suddenly. At first, the thunder sounds distant and muffled, the lightning seems feeble and removed. In the time it takes to unload canoes and pitch camp, the sky may have darkened and trees started to sway wildly, buffeted by high winds on the violent perimeter of the storm. The winds are often followed by a brief, savage hailstorm as lightning splits the sky and plunges into the woods and water. Within minutes the awesome drama will have passed, leaving the forest in a wash of steady, gentle rain.

Excellent campsites, free of litter, are scattered throughout the Boundary Waters. Most sites will have a welcoming committee of Canada jays and chipmunks, and often red squirrels as well. The chipmunks usually hover at the edges of activity, darting up and down trees or across the ground with tense, short rushes. There is nothing timid about the Canada jay, otherwise known as the "whiskey jack" or "camp robber." Like all of its jay cousins, the whiskey jack is an inquisitive, often comical bird, apparently convinced that man wanders into the wilderness to provide it with tidbits of food. In the thick forests of the North Country, songbirds are more often heard than seen. The melodic outpourings of hermit thrushes and white-throated sparrows are their way of defining territory.

At dusk, the pace of animal life quickens. Feeding pike

and bass splash in reedy shallows. Muskrats emerge from their dens of cattails and aquatic grasses. A rustling back in the foliage might be caused by any number of animals, including white-tailed deer, black bear, raccoon, wolverine, otter, and Canadian lynx. On rare occasions, one may hear the howling of timber wolves — a drawn-out *owoo-oo-oo*, or shorter yelps and wails. The timber wolf once ranged throughout most of the United States, but it has been shot, trapped, and poisoned until there are perhaps no more than fifty animals remaining outside of Alaska and Minnesota. An estimated one thousand wolves roam northern Minnesota, hunting deer and moose in couples or in packs which may have more than a dozen wolves.

Prior to a hunt or other activity, members of a pack have been observed to come together for a session of animated muzzle-touching and tail-wagging. On the trail, they tend to string out in single file, usually with the dominant male in the lead. When the pack does pull down a deer or moose, ravens usually flap down to share the feast. Wolves rarely seem to resent this intrusion; indeed, the gray canines and glossy black birds seem to enjoy each other's company. When wolves scamper about in play, as they often do, ravens may linger to watch the activity. If a wolf playfully charges a raven, the bird will take to flight, yet may drop back to the same place as soon as the wolf bounds off to do mock battle with one of its fellows. Although cautious, wolves are curious animals. In the North Country, people gifted at imitating wolf howls have drawn wolves to the very edge of their campsites. Contrary to the traditions of the Far North thriller, wolves have never been known to make an unprovoked attack upon humans in North America.

The old 275-mile *voyageur* route between Lake Superior and International Falls on Rainy Lake now defines the border between Canada and the United States. For the *voyageurs* this was an arduous trip made at maximum speed in heavily loaded canoes; a canoeist today can enjoy the beauty of this remarkable chain of lakes and short rivers at leisure, and travel lightly by arranging to pick up fresh supplies at Gunflint, Basswood, and Crane lakes. From Grand Portage on Lake Superior, a nine-mile trail winds between lichen-covered rocks and thick strands of pine and fir.

Beyond the overgrown mounds which mark the site of Fort Charlotte, built in the late eighteenth century, the route leads up the shallow Pigeon River to the 69-foot plunge of Partridge Falls, and finally reaches the Laurentian Divide by way of several lakes and ponds, some of which are mantled with white water lilies. At the divide, 1551 feet above sea level and 949 feet above Lake Superior, the novice *voyageurs*, called "pork eaters," would be initiated as "Nor-westers" with a ceremony which included vows, a christening with water shaken from a cedar bough, and a boisterous consumption of rum.

Scenic and historical as the route from Grand Portage to the Laurentian Divide may be, few canoeists take it. A nine-mile uphill hike with a canoe on one's head can be less than recreational. Gunflint Lake, a short distance from the divide, is reached by forest road, and canoeists following the *voyageur* route usually put in there. Between Gunflint Lake and Knife Lake, a distance of some 25 miles, the route passes through a variety of waterways — deep rockbound lakes, marshy ponds, stretches of quiet river as well as tumbles of whitewater which can be portaged. The forest along this stretch is largely virgin. In places, berry bushes fill openings in the forest cover; depending upon the season, passing travelers can gorge themselves upon gooseberries, wild strawberries, blackberries, raspberries, blueberries, or currants. Other edible wild plants of the Boundary Waters Canoe Area are lamb's quarters, chickweed, dandelion, shepherd's purse, trillium, and plantain.

Much of the country west of Knife Lake is covered with second growth timber. Between 1895 and 1930 almost a third of what is now the Boundary Waters Canoe Area was logged out. In the early days of North Country settlements, most of the logging was both rapacious and careless. Piles of slash were left lying in the woods, tinder for devastating fires. In 1871, fire swept through a forest of Wisconsin pine covering an area as large as the state of Delaware. Yet fire was a threat to the forests long before the logging era. Father Jean-Pierre Aulneau, a missionary, canoed the *voyageur* route in 1735 and noted that from Lake

Superior to Lake of the Woods he frequently passed "through fire and a thick stifling smoke" without "even once catching a glimpse of the sun." But jackpine and spruce return so quickly that today it is often hard to tell where the old fires and logging operations occurred.

Basswood Lake, northeast of Ely, sprawls all over the map; it appears to be a confederation of long, narrow bays rather than a single lake. At one time or another during the fur trapping era, several companies had trading posts on the lake. The traders obtained furs, birchbark canoes, fish and occasionally a wife from the Indians, while the Indians received traps, axes, knives and various geegaws of little practical use from the traders. Distant as Basswood Lake is from any ocean, innumerable gulls nest upon its small islands during July.

The sinuous Basswood River, which contains falls and rapids, drains the lake. Close to where this waterway enters Crooked Lake, a rock bearing Indian paintings and chipped designs looms above the water. Alexander MacKenzie, who discovered the river which now bears his name, canoed past this rock in the latter part of the eighteenth century, but failed to notice the rock art. He did, however, comment upon another curious sight in his journal.

Within three miles of the last portage is a remarkable rock, with a smooth face, but split and cracked in different parts, which hang over the water. Into one of its horizontal chasms a great number of arrows have been shot, which is said to have been done by a war party of the Nadowasis or Sioux, who have done much mischief in this country, and left these weapons as a warning to the Chebois [Chippewa] or natives, that, notwithstanding its lakes, rivers, and rocks, it was not inaccessible to their enemies.

By way of defiance, as well as a test of marksmanship, the Chippewa fired their own arrows into the cleft. The arrows have long since vanished, but the rock art is remarkably well preserved. There are beautifully executed paintings of suns, moons, men, moose, loons, and what appear to be pelicans. From their uniform level above the water, it would appear that they were created by men or women standing in canoes. Fingers were probably used as brushes, and colors were derived from natural, uncomplicated sources: hematite for red, soot for black, and clay for white. The durability of the paintings suggests that a remarkable binding agent was used, perhaps bear grease, beeswax, blood, fish oil, white from gull's eggs, or a combination of such ingredients. The rock art here, as at other sites in the region, is mostly between five hundred and one thousand years old.

In Crooked Lake, a few miles from these pictographs, I once hooked a smallmouth bass which almost dragged me out of my canoe. When finally landed, it weighed better than thirteen pounds. As they have for the last three hundred years, Chippewa Indians still fish these waters and hunt the moose which range through the woods. At the time of Maple Moon in the spring, clans of Chippewa gather to boil maple syrup in kettles, rendering a sugar which can be stored and later mixed with water and wild rice, dried corn, berries, beans, or chestnuts. Maple Moon is a time of feasting and celebration. Some Chippewa villages in this region are still only accessible by canoe or float plane.

Curtain Falls, at the western end of Crooked Lake, is a thundering avalanche of water. It is not the highest falls in America, nor the largest, but certainly one of the most beautiful. There was once a lodge here, dismantled after the wilderness area was established. All that remains is foundation rubble, half submerged in berry vines. Like the Chippewa, the modern visitor to this region must pass through it relatively unencumbered, expecting only what food and shelter can be packed in his canoe.

Beyond Curtain Falls, the *voyageur* route passes through a seemingly endless domain of water, rock, and forest, where bald eagles nest and place names evoke their own poetry — Bottle Portage, Lac-la-Croix, Loon River, Vermilion Narrows, Namakan Lake, Kettle Falls, Rainy River. The *voyageurs*, seeking pelts, found in this northern land a maze of rivers and lakes that stretched as far as their strength could carry them before the last flocks of geese had passed overhead and ice stiffened against the banks. For modern man who also seeks the wilderness, this is also true.

137

Water and land interlock like a gigantic jigsaw puzzle at Lac la Croix, close to the western edge of the Boundary Waters Canoe Area. From the 1730's until the late nineteenth century the islet-studded lake was an important link in a three-thousand-mile fur trading artery which stretched from Montreal to isolated posts in the Rocky Mountains and onto the treeless reaches of the Canadian Arctic.

Although the route of the voyageurs passed through an interconnected system of rivers and lakes, occasional stretches of fast water, such as Wheel-barrow Falls on the Basswood River (left), necessitated short portages. Such portages are less demanding of modern-day canoeists, with their light-weight vessels, than they were for the voyageurs, who had to tote 40-foot-long birchbark canoes and 180-pound packs.

White-faced hornets (above right) perch upon the surface of their nest, which dangles from a tree branch like some exotic variety of fruit. The ruffled surface of the nest, which attracted the attention of the photographer near Moose Lake, is associated with this species of hornet (Vespula maculata).

Below right, the action of waves has stripped the bark from this lakeshore tree and has ground pebbles into rounded shapes. In the Boundary Waters Canoe Area, steady winds or sudden squalls can quickly generate sizable waves on the larger lakes.

140–141. A fragrant water lily floats upon the placid surface of the channel connecting Kawishiwi Lake and Square Lake. Numerous ponds in the Boundary Waters Canoe Area are entirely filmed over by the fast-growing aqueous plants. Northern and walleyed pike, bass, and large, villainous-looking muskellunge lurk in the shade provided by the broad lily pads.

Wild sasparilla (above left) grows from a tree bole in a grove of hemlocks. The dried roots of the plant are used as a tonic or flavoring. Other useful or edible plants in the Boundary Waters Canoe Area include various berries, mushrooms, cattail roots, and the leaves of ostrich fern, lamb's quarters, marsh marigold, chicory, shepherd's purse, and trillium.

As if seeking accent for her bright green coloration, a female katydid perches on a red mushroom (below left). At the end of summer, when katydids reach maturity and mate, a variety of mushrooms seem to spring up almost overnight. The insect's abdomen is swollen with eggs.

At right, the approach of autumn is signaled by the reddening of floating water shields on Baptism River. This plant flourishes in still ponds or slowly moving waterways whose bottoms are either sandy or covered with decomposing vegetation.

At left, still dripping after the passage of a rain shower, tamaracks fringe a marshy waterway in the vicinity of Finland, Minnesota. Unlike most conifers, tamaracks shed needles in autumn and are able to adapt to the extremely low winter temperatures of the region.

Wild strawberries (right) are found throughout the Boundary Waters Canoe Area, blooming from April to June. In addition to strawberries, canoeists can forage gooseberries, raspberries, blackberries, blueberries, cloud berries, cowberries, and currants. The voyageurs, racing against the seasons, usually had to be content with pemmican — a mixture of fat, dried buffalo meat and berries.

145

146–147. Sunset over Windego Bay, Isle Royal National Park. Returning from the far-flung trading posts of the Canadian Rockies and the Far North, their canoes filled with bales of fur, voyageurs frequently paused in one of the tranquil bays of Isle Royale before venturing out onto the vast heaving reaches of Lake Superior.

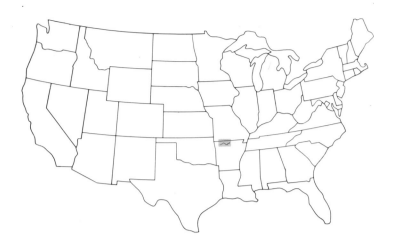

Photographs by George Silk

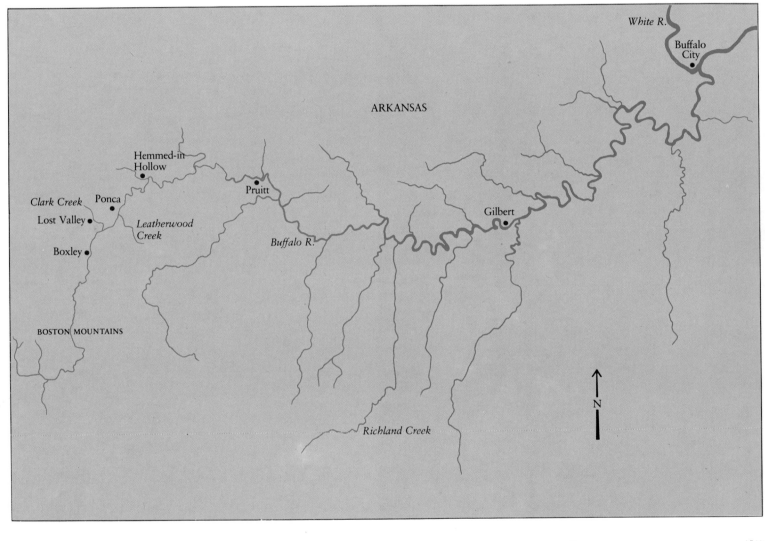

White R.

Buffalo
City

ARKANSAS

Hemmed-in
Hollow

Clark Creek   Ponca

Pruitt

Lost Valley   *Leatherwood*
Creek

Gilbert

Buffalo R.

Boxley

BOSTON MOUNTAINS

Richland Creek

N

0   15 Mi

0   15 Km

The Buffalo

From the air, the Ozark Mountains are not dramatic. There are no peaks or sharp ridges of bare rock, but rather a succession of thickly wooded, gentle swells. At their crest, in the Boston Mountains of northwestern Arkansas, the Ozarks are still less than 2,600 feet in elevation, puny beside the Appalachians, let alone the Rockies or Sierra Nevada. Yet as a hiker soon discovers, this rumpled upland is extremely rugged country. The 148-mile-long Buffalo River, which rises in the Boston Mountains, has carved a steep-sided valley out of limestone and sandstone. The dense foliage of this region tends to mask the intricate play of water and rock up side canyons.

Headwater tributaries such as Terrapin Branch, Clark Creek, and Leatherwood Creek begin in remote, isolated pockets where springwater trickles over limestone rims to drop in soft curtains — not quite waterfalls, and barely more than mist. Gathering swiftly, the rills feed slender, secret pools shaded by dogwood and the giant leaf clusters of umbrella maple. Delicate scrimshaws of rock and high, misty waterfalls are all but buried beneath a rampant growth of oaks, sassafras, vines, ferns, and flowering shrubs. Rainbow Falls, above Edgeman Creek, is only a few miles from a farming settlement, yet was not discovered and named until hikers came upon them in the 1960's.

Below the bedrock, strange and wonderful formations decorate the sunless chambers of numerous caverns. It is this sense of intimacy and of mystery, perhaps, which has given rise to the whimsical nomenclature of the small, half-abandoned settlements one finds up on the rocky benches and in the hollows of this country — Magic Springs, Bug Scuffle, Blue Eye, Evening Shade, Lick Skillet, and Morning Star. The names of wild growing things have an equal lilt — pussy toes, butter and eggs, bastard toad flax, mad dog, Johnny-jump-up, old man of the earth, rattlesnake master, wake robin...

The Buffalo River itself is both intimate and subtle. In some stretches it rushes through shoals and tears at the bases of tall, multi-colored bluffs; in others it lingers as long mint-green pools where turtles bask on logs in the sun. Willow and sycamore crowd the banks, and slopes are splashed with the vivid colors of wildflowers such as fir pink, azalea redbud and celandine poppy. In the early mornings a thin mist often lingers over the water, and a variety of birds "holler a man out of bed," as the local inhabitants say. Fireflies flash in the night as bullfrogs and their smaller cousins pipe the choruses.

When white men first came here, less than two hundred years ago, game was plentiful. Herds of bison grazed head-high bluestem grass on the upland prairies. Countless deer browsed the sidehills and bear denned under limestone ledges. One traveler reported seeing thousands of squirrels swimming across the Buffalo River. The first arrivals, hunters and trappers occasionally skirmished with the Osage, who considered the region their hunting grounds. Nevertheless, they soon began to fill crude boats with buffalo and bear hides, drifting down the Buffalo River into the White River, the White into the Mississippi, and on down to the lively markets of New Orleans. By the time settlers had begun to drift up along the river with their high-wheeled wagons, the bison were all but completely killed off, and both the Osage and the professional white hunters had moved on westward.

The settlers built cabins of log and stone, and attempted to coax crops from the stony soil. For entertainment, some of them brought fiddles; others carried marbles made out of limestone and baked clay. In Ozark hamlets like Blue Eye, men still flick their taws, shooters, at ringmen in a ten-foot square with all the dignity and aplomb of billiard sharks. Yet good soil was limited. It was overworked, and depleted, and many of the settlers, like the buffalo hunters before them, moved westward.

Because its resources were neither extensive nor highly profitable, much of the Buffalo River country has reverted to more of a wild state than it was a century ago. Beaver, for example, were extinct in the region by 1895; they now flourish. Squirrel and opossom, once all but hunted out, have increased in number and are a staple food of the rural people who remain.

The Buffalo is the only major undammed stream in the Arkansas Ozarks. In the early 1960s the Army Corps of Engineers proposed to back up the middle Buffalo with a dam. The Ozark Society vigorously opposed the project, and conservation organizations across the nation rallied behind them. The late Supreme Court Justice William O. Douglas remarked that: "This river is too beautiful to die." In 1972, Congress designated the Buffalo as America's first National River — thus protecting it from dams or irresponsible development.

About half a mile downslope from the summit of Buffalo Knob, highest point in the Ozarks, a trickle of water you can momentarily divert with your hands slips out from under rocks and a bed of leaves. This is the beginning of the Buffalo River. For several miles it tumbles down steep ravines, joined by other rills. By the time it reaches the community of Boxley, it has become a brisk stream flowing through a narrow
150 valley.

Boxley itself is a tranquil scattering of buildings — an old mill, a two-story frame church, an abandoned schoolhouse, and frame farmhouses with porch swings. This is a community where families have known each other for generations, and time is measured by marriages and deaths, as well as news, both triumphant and troubling, of youngsters who have emigrated to distant cities. Down by pools of the river, where dogwoods stretch limbs of pink and white blossoms in the spring, the community sometimes gathers for a baptism or a fish fry.

Clark Creek, which flows into the Buffalo near Boxley, is only three miles long, yet drops some 1,200 feet from its source. The banks are steep and covered with thick undergrowth; early settlers, curious as to its source, had to wade up the stream. They discovered the spectacular alcove now known as Lost Valley, which contains caves, a natural bridge, and an overhang whose immense slab roof is half the size of a football field. Waterfalls leaped from scalloped cliffs 200 feet high.

For more than a century Lost Valley remained a local attraction. Then, in 1945, Glenn Green, the Arkansas Publicity Director, decided to run down the rumors he had heard of a beautiful hidden valley in the Boston Mountains. Driving through the mountains, he had to inquire at several crossroad stores before he found someone who could direct him. After passing the natural bridge, and a series of waterfalls, he and his companions scrambled up a steep slope and entered a cave, where they heard the roar of yet another falls, apparently deep within the cave. As he reported, "We had crawled from 200 feet back from the mouth of the cave when the passage narrowed to a still lower crevice. As we squirmed through, then at last could stand erect, we were nearly overcome with the spectacle. Here we were, deep within a mountain, probing with flashlights around the walls of a circular room perhaps 40 feet high. Over a ledge near the ceiling came a splendid waterfall."

Indians inhabited Lost Valley more than a thousand years ago. From beneath the huge rock overhang, now called Cob Cave, archeologists have recovered miniature corncobs, pieces of gourds, sunflower seeds, and basket fragments.

Beyond Lost Valley, at Ponca, State Highway 74 swings across the Buffalo on a low concrete bridge. Canoeists put in here if the water level is right; less than six inches of space between the bridge and the water indicates a dangerous trip, more than eighteen inches signals marginal boating — much bumping into rocks and dragging of canoes. There is usually a large school of bluegill underneath the bridge. My son, Sean, once waded into the pool with a dropline which he tossed out at shoulder level; the bluegill had little interest in his worms that afternoon, but they brushed against his calves and softly nipped them. Downriver we saw schools of minnows skipping out of the water like silver pebbles, possibly fleeing one of the small-mouth bass for which the river is noted. A variety of aquatic snakes are found in the Buffalo, including cottonmouth moccasins.

The Buffalo, especially in the 25-mile stretch from Ponca to Pruitt, threads its way beneath large and colorful bluffs. Some, such as the Castle, present water-chiseled, nearly vertical faces where few plants find purchase. Others are draped with masses of woodbine, which blaze with shades of red and yellow in autumn. There are bluffs the color of old bones, powder blue bluffs, and rock faces stained orange from the seep of iron-bearing water. Bee Bluff, a little below Ponca, takes its name from a daring raid made upon a honey cache in 1916. Local people had observed bees coming and going from a high crevice for decades before two youths constructed an eighty-foot ladder and killed the bees by stuffing burning rags and sulfur into their natural hive. The narrow entrance of the crevice was dynamited. Streams of honey poured down the face of the cliff, and the boys lowered bucketful after bucketful of wild honey still in its comb to the excited crowd below.

Bees are as plentiful as ever along the Buffalo River, as might be expected in an area where there are over eight hundred species of flowering plants. Bears are not. In his *History of Newton County,* Walter Lackey provides a haunting account of how the last bear was killed in the area about a century ago: "...with an army of hunters in pursuit, the bear was chased through Leatherwood Cove, across the river...down the river to Roark Bluff, from there to the top of Bee Bluff

where the bear made a halt, and sat hugging a cedar tree....One of the hunters shot the bear and it tumbled over a cliff."

Big Bluff, a couple of bends downriver from Bee Bluff, looms more than 500 feet above the river — the highest scarp in south-central United States. The Goat Trail tracks along a ledge high up on the face of the bluff. After winding between knobby, twisted junipers, the trail narrows to an exposed balcony from which firm-footed hikers can gaze at the river 350 feet directly below. Possibly the path was initially tramped out by the semi-wild goats which roam throughout the Buffalo River country; more likely it was a game trail enlarged by human passage. Farm folk traveling between Buffalo River hamlets used trails because the ruggedness of the country made wagon roads impractical.

Below Big Bluff, one can unknowingly drift right by the entrance to Hemmed-in Hollow, where the highest single-jump waterfall between the southern Appalachians and the Rockies leaps over a limestone lip.

In 1917 Colonel William O'Neill built a summer cabin in this isolated niche of fern and falling water, wild plum and hummingbirds. He abandoned the place after three years, but the romanticism of the setting must have rubbed off on his daughter, Rose, who later became a poet and sculptor, and also invented the Kewpie doll. A short distance downriver, Indian Creek flows into the Buffalo. No one has ever presumed to build a trail up this tight willow-tangled waterway, much less a cabin. Sections of the stream flow underneath cobbles of the streambed, yet there are also unexpected waterfalls and an elegant natural bridge.

The Upper Buffalo has a number of shoals such as Wreckin' Rock, Grey Rock Rapids, Close Call Curve, and Crisis Curve that have scraped a good deal of paint from canoe bows and ejected many of their occupants. Below Pruitt, however, the river begins to become gentler. Bass lurk in deep jade pools. Dragonflies hover over the still water and dart back into the woods where black-eyed Susans, Dutchman's breeches, and the white blossoms of the serviceberry push up between oaks, beeches, and silver maple. In places, springs push out of the limestone bluffs, and the water is almost hidden by layers of thick green ferns and mosses. Springs issue 151 from porous limestone layers all through this country. Some linger in small pools which are surrounded by watercress, needle spikerush, waterweed, millfoil and starwort.

The river broadens, fed by streams such as the Little Buffalo River, Big and Cove creeks, Cane Branch, and Rough Edge Hollow. It passes through the Boone formation, a layer of rock hundreds of feet deep. Spectacular ravines have been created where underground water has dissolved and honeycombed the rock until it collapsed. This is cave country. Confederate soldiers extracted potassium nitrate for gunpowder from the floor of Bat Cave. Copperhead Sink is a seventy-foot vertical shaft. Snakes crawl about in the perpetual gloom of the bottom, apparently living on frogs which fall into the pit from time to time.

In the 1830s two frontiersmen followed a bear down a rubble-strewn shaft which opened into a huge chamber. The bear charged, knocking his pursuers' pine torches to the damp cave floor, where they sizzled out. In the absolute darkness of the underworld, the brothers, incredible as it seems, were able to kill the bear with knives. Later, they returned to explore the wonders of the extensive cavern—Diamond Cave—they had discovered. In Haunted Cave, it is said, one can sometimes hear the eerie tunes of a fiddler who once wandered into it and never returned.

Outside of a handful of rustic hamlets like Bosley, Hasty, and Gilbert, few people live on the Buffalo itself. Yet on clear autumn afternoons one may see smoke curling up from the chimney on an unseen cabin in some hollow high above the river. One evening, camped across from the narrow saddle which separates the Buffalo from Richland Creek, I heard a pack of hounds baying along a distant ridge. Somewhere up there, I knew there would be some hunters seated around a fire, reading the nature and progress of the hunt from the calls of their individual dogs.

Close to a high bluff appropriately named the Lookoff, the Buffalo makes a wide loop. Here, in late summer of a dry year the river vanishes, taking a three-mile underground shortcut to reappear as White Springs

on the other side of the bend. The springs, colder than the river, issue from cracks in the riverbed. In low water it is a strange experience to stand over one of these vents and feel the chill water writhe up and around your body. Two long loops from White Springs, the river glides into Rye Bottom. From here, one can scramble up a steep hillside to Peter Cave, once occupied by Indians. From this vantage, canoes seem dwarfed, mere toys, and the fast water of Bucking Shoals glistens in the sunlight. Beyond, the blue and orange fortress of Red Bluff dominate the next bend of the river.

In its final thirty-two miles, the Buffalo pushes past wooded ridges and distinctive bluffs, such as Elephant Head, which appears to dip a stone trunk into the water. As on the upper river near Ponca, there is a feeling of wildness to the country. Less than fifty people live in one hundred square miles of forested hill and hollow. The river plunges through several shoals which are overhung by willows, their roots having been torn loose by high water.

Although cattle range wherever there is good bottomland, most of the farms close to the river are deserted; golden honeysuckle drapes rusty hayrakes and bats roost in sagging barns. Here, perhaps more than on any other section of the Buffalo, one has a sense of the land being returned to itself. Gray squirrels chatter in the trees. Whippoorwills call in the evenings. One rounds a bend of the river to enter a pool where flocks of teal, coots, and shoveler ducks fan and kick their way up from the water. Tree branches and saplings have been gnawed by beaver, even though in this relatively mild climate the animals live in bankside burrows rather than pond lodges. The Buffalo finally opens into the White River, up which canoeists should paddle about half a mile along the left bank so that they can angle across to the hamlet of Buffalo City, the most practical point to leave the river.

Few people who voyage the Buffalo fail to return or at least dream of it. Long after one has gone back to a world of lawns, concrete, and traffic jams, images of a scarlet cardinal skimming over a mint green pool and the flashes of fireflies against darkness remain in the mind's eye.

153

From its headwaters in the thickly forested Boston Mountains (above), the Buffalo River quickly cuts its way down through layers of porous limestone foundations. Although once extensively logged and homesteaded, much of the river has reverted to semi-wilderness and is considered by many the most beautiful canoeing stream in middle America.

154–155. Edgeman Creek, a tributary of the upper Buffalo River, gnaws at the base of a limestone outcropping. A short distance downstream the creek plunges over 30-foot-high Rainbow Falls. The headwaters country of the Buffalo is so rugged and buried in rampant vegetation that the falls was virtually unknown until the 1960's.

156–157. Clark Creek, a three-mile-long tributary of the Buffalo, rushes from the opening of a natural bridge which it has gouged through fifty feet of layered limestone. The spectacular caves and waterfalls of Lost Valley, a hidden alcove at the head of Clark Creek, were discovered outside of nearby mountain villages four decades ago.

In early spring, Lost Valley (left) is filled with the roar of water tumbling from ledges and cascading through narrow limestone slots. By midsummer many of the falls are dry and sections of the lower creek vanish beneath boulders and gravel.

Deep within the vaulted rock walls of Lost Valley (right), springwater plummets off limestone ledges and pours out of cave mouths. Tiny corn cobs, sunflower seeds, and fragments of baskets and gourds were left by Indians who lived in one of the caves more than a thousand years ago.

159

160

Leatherwood Creek (left), another tributary of the upper Buffalo, glides past a mossy bank where a purple phlox commonly called Sweet William blooms. Other colorful plants in Buffalo River country include butter and eggs, wake robin, mad dog, old man of the earth, Johnny-jump-up, and rattlesnake master.

At right, falling water is mirrored in a quiet pool on Leatherwood Creek. Each tributary of the Buffalo is unique and has carved its signature into layers of limestone.

161

162–163. The upper Buffalo River is fast and rocky in a number of stretches, but gentles into a quiet pool beneath a slab-sided bluff near the village of Pruitt. Beyond Pruitt the only settlements on the river are the semi-deserted hamlets of Mt. Hersey and Gilbert.

162

As below, every bluff
beside the Buffalo has its
distinctive shape, hue, and
design, created by a
combination of rock
strata, erosion, and
minerals which stain the
rock faces as seep water
evaporates. While some
bluffs rise sharply from
the river, others have
narrow, talus slopes at
their bases.

164

166–167. *The base cliffs of Big Bluff, as seen from the Goat Trail, loom above the jade flow of the Buffalo River. The steep, narrow trail, which might have more appeal to the semi-wild goats which roam the Buffalo River country than to a human, ascends some 350 feet above the river. Big Bluff itself is over 500 feet high.*

166

A two-hundred-foot-high strand of falling water (below), whose base sways in the wind, drops with lofty grace into the eroded amphitheatre of Hemmed-in Hollow. Only a mile from the Buffalo River, this is the highest single-jump waterfall between the Rockies and Appalachians. Dogwood (below right) blooms near a stream.

In the Ozarks, where waterfalls are commonplace, occasionally a stream will bore a hole through the overhang of its lip, creating what is locally known as a glory hole (right). Innumerable rills and streams have carved a scrimshaw of rock formations throughout the region.

169

170–171. *A brace of falls plunges into a clear, chill pool at Devil's Fork in the upper Richmond Valley. This part of the Richmond Valley, which is heavily wooded, is visited only by an occasional hunter or hiker. The lower valley broadens before opening into the Buffalo and contains a scattering of abandoned cabins.*

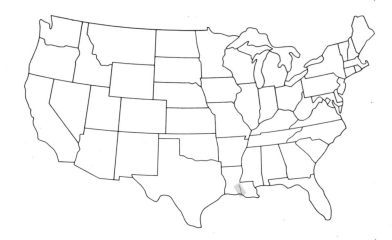

Photographs by Yva Momatiuk and John Eastcott

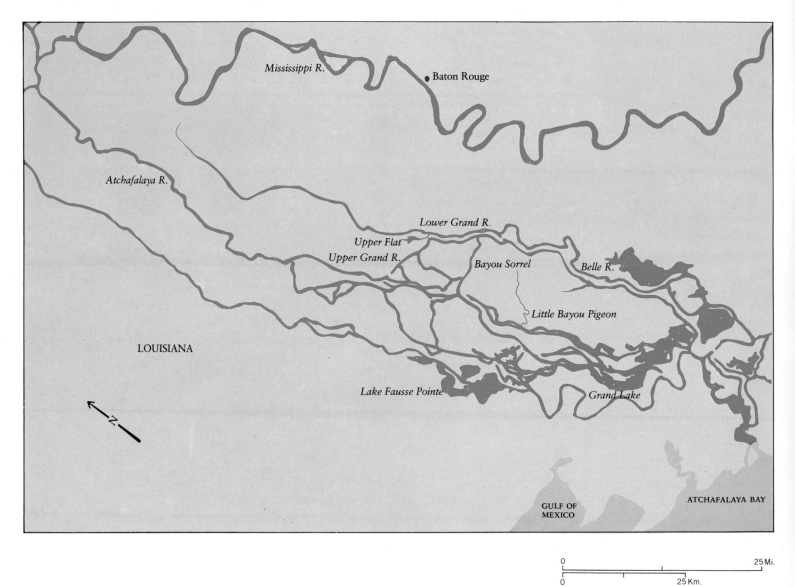

Mississippi R.

Baton Rouge

Atchafalaya R.

Lower Grand R.

Upper Flat

Upper Grand R.

Bayou Sorrel

Belle R.

Little Bayou Pigeon

LOUISIANA

Lake Fausse Pointe

Grand Lake

N

GULF OF
MEXICO

ATCHAFALAYA BAY

0   25 Mi.

0   25 Km.

The Atchafalaya

An estimated eight hundred years ago, some of the Mississippi River's flow began to slip away from the main channel about forty miles northwest of present-day Baton Rouge, Louisiana. The gentle currents soon worked their way through the hardwood forests of the Atchafalaya Basin, eventually creating North America's largest river basin swamp. During the early days of settlement in Louisiana, the Atchafalaya River was little more than a wide, sluggish stream, in some places covered from bank to bank with rafts of logs so thickly clustered and matted with vegetation that cattle could be driven across them.

Convenient as these log jams might be as natural bridges, they made navigation all but impossible, and by the mid-1870s work crews had broken them up. Gradually, the main channel of the Atchafalaya as well as the myriad bayous and overflow lakes began to accept more and more Mississippi River water. After a disastrous Mississippi flood in 1927, it was decided to turn the Atchafalaya Basin into an escape channel for rampaging flood waters. The U.S. Army Corps of Engineers dredged the main channel of the river and levees were constructed beside it. The Atchafalaya claimed still more of the Mississippi's flow. Had not floodgates been constructed to control the Mississippi River water entering the Atchafalaya, most of the "Big Muddy" might now be moving through this shorter route to the sea, leaving the ports of Baton Rouge and New Orleans isolated in a quiet bayou. As it is, thirty per cent of the Mississippi's volume reaches the Gulf of Mexico through the Atchafalaya.

The Atchafalaya Basin is a region of contrasts. At the northern end, much of the original hardwood forest has been axed down to make way for pasture and soybean fields. Farther south, Cajun fishermen pole narrow pirogues through drowned cypress forests. The Atchafalaya River itself has been aptly described as "one of the shortest, deepest, most treacherous rivers in the world." Three-story-high tugboats with blunt snouts push strings of barges up and down the tawny flow, passing between banks of muck thrown up by dredges, where puny willows attempt to gain purchase. Yet a mile or two away is an intimate, shallow waterway where a variety of birds wing from the cypress, sycamore, and tupelo branches which seal off the sky. One can find deep, muffled forests where a stick breaking underfoot sounds like a gunshot and hidden lakes where mullet may leap right into your boat.

The Atchafalaya hardwood swamp is some seventy miles long and seventeen miles wide. It supports a diversity and volume of wildlife which is considered to be greater than that of Florida's Everglades. In late winter and spring the river quickly swells with runoff, carrying topsoil and nutrients ranging from microscopic leaf fragments to entire trees—all of it coming from middle America. It spills back into the swamp, providing an ideal nursery for minute organisms, shrimp, crawfish, tadpoles, salamanders, river crabs,

173

and turtles. As the waters recede in late summer and fall, the maturing water creatures provide food for larger fish, raccoons, river otters, and fishing birds. A profusion of greenery springs up from the rich, damp soil, nourishment for swamp rabbits, squirrels, nutria, beaver, and other small mammals, who in turn are prey for fox and bobcat.

Graceful, snow-white egrets stalk shallow waterways, pausing from time to time to stab their long beaks at fish, frogs, or crustaceans. During the spring nesting season, hundreds of egrets occupy one of the swamp rookeries, flapping with an oddly ponderous grace between food sources and nests. The parents' catch, stored in its long neck and stomach, is regurgitated into the beaks of the hungry chicks. The young birds themselves occasionally fall prey to alligators, snapping turtles, raccoons, and hawks.

The crawfish is perhaps the most celebrated creature of the Atchafalaya. In other parts of the country the small lobster-like crustaceans are usually called crayfish or crawdads, and are regarded as little more than entertainment for the small boys who catch them in streams. Yet in the Atchafalaya swamp, crawfish are not taken lightly. Folks drive in from as far away as New Orleans to set up camp and catch them in nets baited with chunks of meat. These delicacies, from three to seven inches long, are boiled in a pot along with seasonings. And for the people who earn their livelihood from the swamp, crawfishing is a serious business.

After the mating season of the crawfish in May or June, the female digs a burrow 24 to 40 inches deep into the viscous mud beside a stream. She lays her eggs in September; until the eggs are hatched some fifteen days later the egg cluster, resembling a blueberry, is attached to the underside of her tail. Although herons and other birds, mink, raccoons, and fish all feast on the young crawfish, the sheer volume of hatchlings assures that vast quantities of them will grow to a size appreciated by human predators.

The future of the Atchafalaya wetlands is a matter of heated controversy. Each year, as a large part of the swollen flood of the Mississippi River pours into the Atchafalaya Basin, a new layer of sediment is laid down. Local landowners regard this inexorable natural process with satisfaction; they envision fields of soybean and sugar cane where stands of cypress now rise from the waters. They would like the Corps of Engineers, which controls the flow of water through the Atchafalaya Basin by means of dredging and levees, to gradually drain the swamp. The second-growth cypress forest is now almost harvestable.

Environmentalists argue that the Corps of Engineers should preserve the swamp by letting the seasonal wash of water through it. Most of the swamp is now in private ownership. A long-range plan developed by several federal and state agencies proposes that the Atchafalaya wetlands be purchased for public use. This plan, currently being discussed in seemingly endless rounds of public hearings, would assure that large portions of the swamp remain in a semi-wilderness state.

One morning, photographer C. C. Lockwood and I canoed down Bayou Sorrel. The bayou is lined with huge, stately cypress which canopy the smaller, sprawling oaks and bitter pecan. Cypress knees thrust out of the water like so many wooden stalagmites upon a flooded cave floor. Botanists are still not completely sure as to the functions of these exposed roots, but it is thought that they not only provide support in the soft swamp but also give the trees access to additional oxygen. Between the end of the Civil War and the 1920s, the virgin cypress forest of the Atchafalaya was logged out; nearly all of today's extensive stands of cypress are second growth.

The wide channel of the bayou was busy that morning. A party of sport fishermen skimmed by in a skiff with outboard motor. A helicopter whirred overhead. The Atchafalaya is an active oil field, with drilling platforms and dredges scattered throughout the swamp. We passed the site of a recent oil exploration. Uprooted trees lay upon a spoilbank of raw, dredged-up earth. Lockwood looked in vain for the channels which are supposed to be cut in such spoilbanks. Without provisions for drainage in low water, portions of the swamp become stagnant and sour.

Abruptly, we left Bayou Sorrel and its bustle to enter a small winding waterway. It was as though we were paddling into a tunnel of trees and airplants. A lush undergrowth—arrowhead, palmetto, alligator weed,

174

elephant ears—crowded the banks. A red-winged blackbird called raucously from a tree limb sheathed with the deep green leaves of resurrection fern.

From time to time we drifted in silence in the slow current, listening to bass jumping in the water. Deep in the swamp, one has a feeling of being in a place of great antiquity and mystery. The gray-green Spanish moss which hangs from oak and cypress trees heightens this mood.

That night, we camped beside a larger bayou where schools of small shad were disturbing the surface of the water, we heard the drawn-out "hoo-hoooo" of a barred owl, soon echoed by several owls calling back and forth. Some of them made harsh croaks. These fierce nocturnal predators actually have eight distinctive calls, yet the last sound heard by most of their prey—small rodents—is the rapid fanning of wings before the strike.

The next day at dawn, a variety of birds greeted the subtle shifts of light from ash to pink to pale whiskey with a yammer and clear, soft songs. By the time the sun was teetering on the horizon, a fisherman had entered the bayou and was grappling up a large hoop net. He shook several flopping catfish and buffalo fish out into his skiff. Some fishermen mark the locations of their nets with floats; others, fearing robbery, use no markers but rely upon natural forms such as prominent trees, and have an uncanny ability to gauge how far the submerged net is from the shore. Many of the people who live off the wildlife of the swamp—through fishing, setting out crawfish traps, and the trapping of nutria, muskrat, and beaver—are descendants of settlers who were driven out of Canada in 1775. Most of them now live in villages at the edge of the swamp, and are known for their spicy dishes, distinctive folk music, and spirited *fais-dodos*—dances which are attended by entire families and frequently last until dawn.

After breakfast, we canoed along the shore of a large, shallow lake, stopping briefly at a hummock of relatively dry land which was blanketed with a thick layer of clamshells. Freshwater clams and mussels are found throughout the Atchafalaya, but this white mound, like many others scattered throughout the swamp, dates back to eighteenth century feasts of the Chitimacha Indians. The Chitimacha were hunting and fishing in the swamp when the first Frenchmen entered it. For a time, relationships were cordial, and the Indians freely shared their knowledge of the swamp and its resources with the newcomers. As everywhere else in America, however, some of the white men regarded the Indians as less than human and savagely abused their hospitality. By way of retaliation, Indians killed a French missionary and three companions in 1706, precipitating a war in which the tribe was nearly annihilated. Descendants of the survivors live today in Charenton at the edge of the swamp—the only federal Indian reservation in Louisiana.

Before leaving the swamp that evening, we explored a long, shallow bayou where schools of minnows and small bass darted away at the approach of the canoe. Our progress was finally barred by a bed of water hyacinth which covered the surface of the bayou from bank to bank and stretched off down the waterway until it turned a distant bend. A number of bayous and small lakes in the Atchafalaya are choked with this plant, an orchid-like native of South America with an awesome ability to reproduce itself. In languid waterways such as those of the swamp, water hyacinths can double their number every two weeks. Apparently this hardy plant was first brought to Louisiana by the Japanese delegation to the International Cotton Exposition of 1884. They passed out the lovely purple blossoms as souvenirs. Most were discarded, but the seeds, carried by wind and birds, were soon sprouting on waterways throughout southern Louisiana.

As early as 1897 the Corps of Engineers attempted to eradicate the intruder by hiring gangs of men to rip up the plants with pitchforks and throw them onto the banks. In addition, a sternwheeler equipped with conveyor belt and shredder chewed its way down the middle of blocked bayous, spitting out the pulp of the offending plant. Within a year, streams thus purged seemed to be more thickly covered by the beautiful exotic than those which had not been disturbed. Dynamite was tried but with little success. Becoming frustrated, the hyacinth fighters tried flame throwers. Recently, chemicals have kept hyacinths partly under control.

175

On any given weekend, the boat landings at the edge of the Atchafalaya swamp are crowded with automobiles and boat-trailers. Fishermen in skiffs powered by outboard motors and speedboat enthusiasts cruise through a labyrinth of wide, deep bayous and lakes. Yet there are also innumerable bayous which are shallow, have logs just under the surface and tight, narrow bends. C.C. and I had canoed such tranquil waterways. The Atchafalaya also contains a number of forest-rimmed lakes which for much of the year can be entered only by portaging a canoe or poling it across a sill of mud.

Upper Flat, which lies to the north of the well-traveled Grand River, is such a place. One fall afternoon I canoed into Upper Flat with two friends from Baton Rouge. We paddled beside a row of huge cypress stumps, melancholy gray monuments to the logging era. Some of them had decayed into flakes and knobs, giving them a curiously eroded look. Close to the entrance to the lake, as if guarding it, a large red-shouldered hawk perched at the top of a dead cypress. A chattering kingfisher buzzed low over the water. A flock of great blue herons landed softly in some nearby trees. From the water mullet leaped everywhere. We paused, engulfed by growth, listening. Many different species of birds were calling. Back toward the open water, an anhinga—also known as a water turkey or snakebird—wheeled in its languid flight to dive underwater. A fishing bird with webbed feet and a long, serpentine neck, the anhinga is as much at home in the water as in the air. Within arm's reach, a spider dangled gracefully from a strand of its thread which was attached to a warped finger of cypress. A red-tailed hawk sailed overhead as a fish jumped in the narrow gap of water between the duckweed and the shore. The area pulses with life.

Later, we beached and walked back into the high-vaulted forest of cypress upon a spongy turf carpeted with rust-colored needles. The great fluted cypress seemed solid enough, but the smaller trees, such as the slender swamp privet, were all bent in the same direction as if from strong currents of water. In the green twilight, I had a sense of being underwater, as this section of forest is during the wet season.

There are no rocks in the swamp, yet as we canoed through a partially submerged cypress grove I made out the angular shape of what appeared to be a huge boulder. Upon closer examination, it proved to be an ancient cabin cruiser, wedged between the moss-hung trees as if in a vise. Periodically, hurricanes sweep up from the Gulf of Mexico and blast through the Atchafalaya at up to 200 miles per hour. Huge patriarchal cypress trees are uprooted and crash down through lesser growth. Other trees are stripped of leaves; branches whirl through the air. Fish are snatched up from the water and numerous terrestrial animals drown.

In the aftermath of such a violent storm, surviving creatures seem in a state of shock for hours, predators and prey forgetting their roles. Bobcats and swamp rabbits, snakes and mice, have been observed to occupy the same hummock of land or floating log without interest in each other. Sometimes there will be an exodus of certain animals from the areas of the swamp most severely damaged. Squirrels, finding oaks purged of their acorns and the nuts gone from pecan trees, may migrate to other areas by the hordes. Bobcats and the gray foxes that prey upon them will often follow. Yet in the long run, a hurricane can be beneficial for some species of wildlife. Although numerous white-tailed deer usually drown during the fury of a hurricane, broken tree limbs provide immediate forage for those who manage to escape to higher ground; and where entire groves of trees have been flattened, underbrush will soon spring up to provide food and shelter for years to come.

My friends and I paddled back to the boat landing at the edge of the swamp in the gathering dusk. The rustling of unseen, nocturnal creatures came from behind a low screen of buttonbush. Fish were still jumping. A sleek body plopped into and under the water from the bank. Mink? Muskrat? It surfaced behind the canoe to reveal the sinuous neck of an anhinga. Back in the dim woods a screech owl emitted a weird, trembling call. As we docked at the boat landing in the dark, I began to understand why so many people feel such strong affection for the Atchafalaya, and why they are so dedicated to its preservation.

177–179. *The setting sun and morning mists (overleaf) provide eerie backdrops to weathered cypress stumps lifting out of Upper Flat Lake in the Atchafalaya Swamp of southern Louisiana. A third of the volume of the Mississippi River flows into the Atchafalaya Basin from floodgates forty miles northwest of Baton Rouge. Over a period of some eight hundred years, the annual sediment-laden floods of the Mississippi have turned the seventy-mile-long floodplain into North America's largest river basin swamp.*

180–181. *Black vultures, attracted by stranded fish, congregate at Upper Flat Lake. Although the falling water level of late summer and autumn traps and kills some fish in drying ponds, it is the seasonal cycle of high and low water which nurtures an extraordinary volume and diversity of marine life. During the late winter and spring, floodwaters deposit rich sediments, which provide nourishment for minute organisms, fish, crayfish, tadpoles, shrimp, salamanders, river crabs, and turtles. As the water recedes, other water creatures provide food for larger fish, raccoons, river otters, and fishing birds.*

182–183. *A torrential rain sweeps through a stand of cypress on Beau Bayou. Most of the virgin cypress of the Atchafalaya wetlands was logged out between the end of the Civil War and 1930. Forests of second-growth cypress are now approaching maturity and conservationists are seeking to preserve them through a plan involving federal and state purchase of private lands for parks and wildlife preserves.*

184

At left, a western cottonmouth coils upon a bed of duckweed in Little Alabama Bayou. Duckweed, which completely covers the surface of some bayous and ponds in the Atchafalaya wetlands, is the smallest flowering plant except for water meal.

A Gulf fritillary butterfly (below left) gathers nectar from napweed. The Atchafalaya Swamp is filled with a diversity of wildlife, ranging from fire-ants to alligators.

A Rana catesbeiana (below), better known as a bullfrog, peers at the world through bulging eyes. The deep, throaty call of such frogs can be heard for half a mile, and the Creole word for the amphibian, ouaouaron, mimics its voice.

185

186–187. A member of the Lantana family. Some early explorers saw the Atchafalaya Basin as a gloomy, threatening place, yet generations of more recent visitors have come to highly value its solitude and prodigal plant and animal life.

A cypress forest (below left) at the edge of Lost Bayou. A network of bayous — some of which are channels, others narrow threads winding between trees and thick undergrowth — connect the myriad ponds and lakes of the Atchafalaya Basin.

At right, beads of water gleam upon foot-wide lotus pads floating upon the surface of Lake Fausse Pointe. Beneath its placid surface, Lake Fausse Pointe, like all of the Atchafalaya Basin ponds, lakes, and bayous, teems with catfish, mullet, buffalofish, bluegill, bass, crappie, freshwater drum, and alligator gar. At dusk, the splashing of leaping fish provides counterpoint to the harsh cries of barred owls.

190–191. *Water hyacinths on Bayou Postillon. This orchidlike native of South America is both beautiful and destructive. The exotic blossoms were distributed as souvenirs at the International Cotton Exposition of 1884, held in New Orleans. Once discarded, the plants soon evidenced their awesome power to survive and reproduce, so thoroughly blanketing waterways throughout southern Louisiana that many of them became barren of subsurface plant and animal life.*

192–193. *Waning light illuminates newly formed islets in Grand Lake, which is at the southern end of the Atchafalaya Basin. The Mississippi, in seeking a shorter route to the sea through the Atchafalaya Basin, is gradually filling with sediment the lakes it once created.*

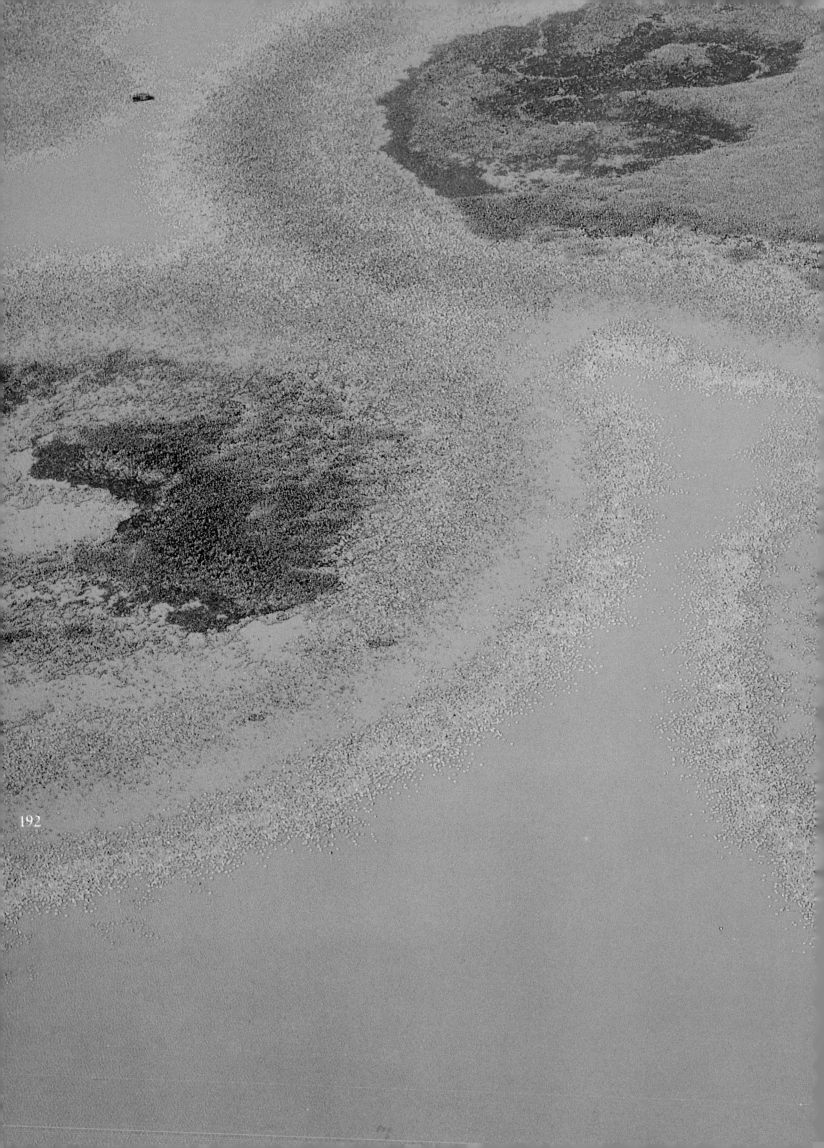

192

194

Much of the splendor of the Atchafalaya Basin resides in plants whose shapes and colors usually go unheeded by people who are in a hurry to get from one place to another. At left, the undersurface of a

Swamp grass (center) seems to catch and celebrate light, while fans of oyster mushroom at right, growing upon a branch of willow, resemble forms of sea life.

Few plants, in terms of design, are more elegantly structured than the palmetto leaf (below). This frond, beside Little Bayou Penchente, seems to draw both sunlight and shadow into its nucleus.

Spider web ladders (bottom), American Island, Atchafalaya Basin. The humid ecosystem of the Atchafalaya Basin nourishes a horde of flying insects, many of whom are caught in the strong, intricate webs of resident spiders.

Fingers of swamp lily push (below right) out from the rich, damp soil of Tiger Island in the Atchafalaya Basin. Here, a variety of flowering plants provides cover for crayfish and other swamp creatures.

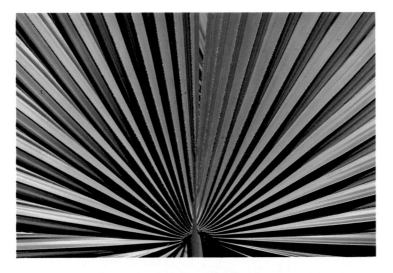

196

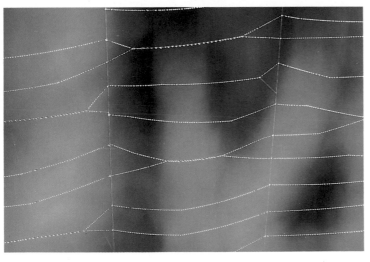

Above, gnarled, fluted columns support a massive cypress rising from the waters of Duck Lake. Botanists are still unsure as to the functions of cypress knees, such as the knob at center foreground, but theorize that they provide additional support and oxygen to the trees.

198–199. Hog Bayou, close to the mouth of the Atchafalaya River, meanders toward the Gulf of Mexico. Close to the Gulf, the swamp forest gives way to vast saltwater marshes which contain a variety of birds and marine life.

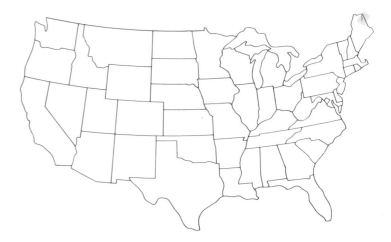

Photographs by Charles Steinhacker

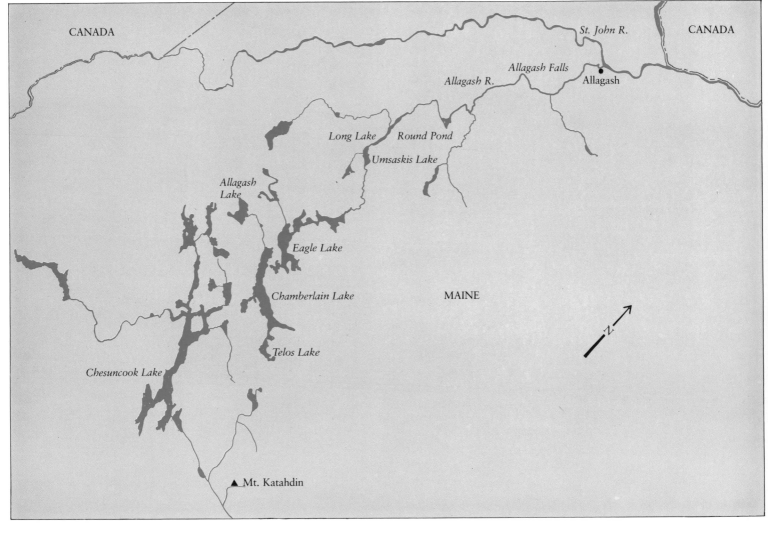

CANADA

St. John R.

CANADA

Allagash Falls

Allagash R.

Allagash

Long Lake   Round Pond

Umsaskis Lake

Allagash
Lake

Eagle Lake

Chamberlain Lake

MAINE

N

Telos Lake

Chesuncook Lake

▲ Mt. Katahdin

0   30 Mi

0   30 Km

The Allagash

In the summer of 1857 Henry David Thoreau canoed through sections of the upper Allagash waterway with a companion and an Indian guide. They fished, gathered plant specimens, swatted blackflies, and marveled at the wildlife, the interconnecting lakes, ponds, and streams, the dense woods. Thoreau wrote:

In the middle of the night, as indeed each time that we lay on the shore of a lake, we heard the voice of the loon, loud and distinct, from far over the lake. It is a very wild sound, quite in keeping with the place and the circumstances of the traveler, and very unlike the voice of a bird. I could lie awake for hours listening to it, it is so thrilling. When camping in such a wilderness as this, you are prepared to hear sounds from some of its inhabitants which will give voice to its wilderness.

In the decades since Thoreau's time, many people have paddled the Allagash, savoring its wildness, and have gone back to their tamer home towns and cities carrying the loon's call in their memories. They returned from an experience with remote waters and woods that was simple yet profound. For most of us, such a place provides a certain spiritual nourishment.

In an effort to preserve the Allagash, the Maine legislature established the 92-mile Allagash Wilderness Waterway in 1966. The lakes, ponds, connecting streams, and the main river itself are protected from development and logging within a corridor of forest, 400 to 800 feet back from the water. Logging is controlled for a mile back from the water. Beyond that, the timber corporations which own the land, including about half the territory of the state, harvest their product as they see fit. From an ardent conservationist's point of view, the wilderness aspect of the Allagash Waterway may seem like a stage prop that merely screens the logging activity.

Nonetheless, the Allagash is still one of America's most beautiful waterways, a gleaming thread hemmed in by magnificent balsam fir and red cedar. A place where moose wade into shallow coves to crop water plants and where loons still call.

Late spring and early autumn are the best times for canoeing on the Allagash. In the spring, brooks swollen with snowmelt tumble and slide into the river and its connecting lakes. A variety of wildflowers push up from meadows carpeted with new grasses, and the hardwood forest of ash, birch, myrtle, and beech echoes with the calls of returning migratory birds such as the hermit thrush, eastern bluebird, and myrtle warbler. Young moose trail their mothers on spindly legs.

By early June, the popularity of the Allagash waterway is painfully apparent. Canoes are scattered all along the waterway and it is often difficult to find a good, unoccupied campsite unless one beaches well before dusk. Canoe traffic falls sharply off after Labor Day and autumn trips can be lovely, although prolonged rains and even snow flurries are calculated risks of the season. Mists often linger over the water and in the woods until mid-morning, giving one a sense of solitude and mystery. Such ground fogs usually burn off to reveal the brilliant yellow and red leaves of the forest.

A voyage down the entire waterway begins at Telos Landing, an overly-used campsite at the roadhead. After passing through Telos Lake and Round Pond one enters long, narrow Chamberlain Lake. Jutting from forested shores are rocky headlands, knuckles of the granite shield which underlies the entire Maine woods. Only twelve thousand years ago the last ice-age glaciers retreated from this country, leaving the granite scraped and gouged, and creating thousands of lakes and ponds by damming watercourses with debris. Here Maine's highest mountains loom to the southeast. As Thoreau commented: "Only seldom bearhaunted mountains, with their great wooded slopes, were visible; where, as man is not, we suppose some other power to be." Upon these mountains the Penobscot Indians hunted bear, squirrels, grouse, and other game. They worshipped Manitou, whose power and mystery were not unlike that which Thoreau felt in gazing at the mountains. The Penobscots usually communicated directly with lesser spirits, one of whose messengers was the loon. In the spring, the tribe netted and speared shad and Atlantic salmon on the spawning runs of these fishes in the headwater lakes and streams. By tradition, when "oak leaves were the size of mouse ears" the Indians planted crops in plots on the lower stretches of the river and, while the crops were maturing, parties journeyed to the sea to kill seal and gather birds' eggs, clams, and lobsters.

The osprey, a handsome fish-eating hawk, can at times be seen flapping high above the waters of the Allagash. When a fish is spotted, it plunges down to snatch up its prey with its talons. From sticks and other plant matter, the osprey constructs a nest which is sturdy enough to support the weight of a man. When the fledglings are old enough to learn to fly, they hop up and down at the edges of these lofty bowers, testing their wings. Sometimes a parent will lure its hesitant offspring into its first flight by flapping close to the nest with a fish which it holds enticingly just out of range.

Scattered throughout the waterway are vestiges of turn-of-the-century logging efforts. At the water's edge in front of Chamberlain Farm lie the fragments of the steamboat *W. H. Marsh*. Built in 1903 to work logs down the lake, it was eventually caught by an early freeze-up. It was cut in half to save the engine, and the following spring a run off destroyed it. The tracks of a three-quarter-mile tramway constructed in 1902 remain at the upper end of Chamberlain Lake, although trees a foot or more in diameter have pushed up between them. Over it, logs were once hauled between Chamberlain Lake and adjoining Eagle Lake. Two abandoned steam locomotives, once used in hauling logs, are cradled by shrubs not far from the tramway. Lock Dam, separating Chamberlain and Eagle lakes, is also a legacy of early logging days, although a comparatively modern structure replaces earlier barricades. Telos and Chamberlain lakes once drained entirely into the Allagash, until enterprising lumbermen threw up dams and dug a short canal by which Allagash waters could be diverted into the Penobscot River system. They could thus drive logs southward to the mills of Bangor, a more profitable market than the one at the mouth of the Allagash.

Allagash Lake drains into the northern end of Lake Chamberlain; it is one of the most beautiful places in the Maine woods. Mallards and black ducks skim across the broad forest-rimmed water, which on calm days reflects an almost perfect mirror image. Back among the spruce and firs one finds twinflowers, witch hazel, dwarf dogwood, and the delicate wild orchid known as lady's slipper. A knowledgeable plant gatherer will find golden chanterelle mushrooms, a gourmet's delight; wild yellow lily, whose bulbs yield an excellent tea; the creeping snowberry, which can be made into one of the most savory of all wild teas. If it is mating season of the ruffed grouse, one may hear the rapid drumming of the male's wings against his body, an amorous overture which sounds like muffled thunder or distant surf. The mottled brown feathers of nesting or brooding grouse give them excellent camouflage against the leaves of the forest floor. Disturbed by a predator such as a fox or a goshawk, a hen will sometimes attempt to draw attention away from her chicks by pretending to have a broken wing. Once the bird, by dint of artful flopping, has drawn the predator some distance from her nest, she will whirr off to safety and soon return to her offspring.

Connecting Allagash Lake to Chamberlain Lake is the six-mile-long Allagash Stream, the course of which is narrow, fast, and rocky. To reach Eagle Lake, Little Allagash Falls must then be portaged. One arm of Eagle Lake is a broad and shallow marsh, excellent habitat for ducks and moose. Protected by law, moose are quite commonly seen along the Allagash, browsing upon water lily and other aquatic plants, or slipping back into thick woods with an ease which belies their rather awkward gait. The marshes of Eagle Lake, adjoining Round Pond and Churchill Lake, are favorite haunts of moose during the blackfly and mosquito season of early summer. These animals, which remain all but completely submerged, experience a misery only somewhat less than that of the canoeist who ventures into the marshes.

Between mosquito and moose the range of life in these marsh-fringed waters is rich and varied. Whitefish, yellow perch, and cusk, a type of catfish, glide through weedy reaches of shallow water, feeding upon insects, worms, smaller fish, and tadpoles. Frogs provide a nightly chorus whose rhythms at times seem as relentless as the sea, at other times as varied as some primitive opera. These are the voices of the common tree frog, Pickering's tree frog, yellow-throated green frog, pickerel frog, bullfrog, and leopard frog.

This is also muskrat country, and the domain of the otter, graceful and sportive. I have had an otter shadow my canoe for two miles, obviously playing, impatient with my laggard pace, much as a porpoise might respond to a boat on the open ocean. Also sometimes seen in these woods are black bear and bobcat, and the so-called Maine wolf (actually a large sub-species of the coyote) which in recent years has wandered down from Canada.

The drawn-out *hoo-oo-oo* of the loon is perhaps the most plaintive of all wilderness sounds. This distinctive cry, usually heard at twilight or after dark, is but one of the loon's voices. These handsome, goose-sized birds also make short cooing sounds when several are gathered together or emit maniacal yodels when the mood strikes them. The loon is an ancient bird, little changed from its ancestors of the Eocene period some 60 million years ago. Loons are splendid divers, propelling themselves underwater with powerful kicks of their webbed feet as they seek out the fish which comprise most of their diet. Loons have been known to stay underwater for as long as three minutes and dive to depths of 180 feet. The birds are heavy, with dense bones, and are able to submerge at will. When threatened, a loon will often swim rapidly away with its neck and bill poking out of the water like a periscope. Loons are strong and graceful in flight, and have been known to speed at up to 60 miles per hour. They cannot, however, become airborne quickly. A loon may sprint across the surface of a lake for a quarter of a mile before lifting off, legs and wings pumping furiously. Parents train their offspring for takeoffs by leading them in lengthy footraces across the surface of the water, events which appear as sportive as they are instructional. The youngsters become accomplished fliers long before ice films the lakes and ponds of the Allagash watershed. With the onset of winter, loons migrate to the Atlantic Ocean, where they remain until the spring thaw.

Below Churchill Dam, Chase Rapids begins, a nine-mile section of challenging water. A damkeeper regulates the flow through the rapids according to the number of canoes coming along on a given day. A recent National Geographic party swamped here with their canoe wedged tightly between boulders. Unruffled, they waded ashore, persuaded the damkeeper to turn off the water, and then were able to retrieve their craft from the dry riverbed. Manipulations aside, when the water is running hard over Chase Rapids, it is a fast and lovely stretch, flanked by a wall of trees which seems little changed from the days when Thoreau ran it. He commented:

It is exceedingly rapid and rocky, and also shallow, and can hardly be considered navigable, unless that may mean that what is launched in it is sure to be carried swiftly down it, though it may be dashed to pieces by the way. It is somewhat like navigating a thunderspout. With commonly an irresistible force urging you on, you have got to choose your own course each moment, between the rocks and shallows, and to get into it, moving forward always with the utmost possible moderation, and often holding on, if you can, that you may inspect the rapids before you.

At Umsaskis Lake, below Chase Rapids, one passes the Wilderness Waterway headquarters. A private road, heavily traveled by logging trucks, bridges the waterway between Umsaskis and Long lakes. Once again, there are reminders that logging has not only been the industry of this region for more than a century but still flourishes today. The first settlers began moving up the St. John River and into the Allagash country in the mid-1830's. They were a hardy breed, mostly of Scotch-Irish or English extraction, who had the strength and determination to clear farm plots from the forest, and then cope with the endlessly stony soil. These "Moosetowners," as they called themselves, were joined by "Herring Chokers," former fishermen from Canada. To augment the returns from their crops and livestock, most of them took to logging for part or much of the year.

The hazards of logging are embedded in names along the Allagash — close to the more northerly Round Pond is Ghost Bar Landing, where a huge pine toppled the wrong way, killing the axman, and McGargle Rocks, below Allagash Falls, which commemorates a logger crushed when a log jam shot out from under him. When loggers were not actually cutting trees or jockeying them down waterways, their diversions were basic and few. In the bunkhouse, a man might be known as a fiddler, a good checker player, or a lively spinner of yarns. Tales were told of encounters with bear, as well as "panthers," as the New Englanders called mountain lions.

The ferocity of the seldom-seen animal known as the fisher was often a point of discussion. Like its larger relative, the wolverine, the fisher is capable of fighting off animals much larger than itself. Although bunkhouse tales would have the fisher a lurking giant, the sleek animals are only slightly larger than a hefty housecat. These fierce loners feed mostly upon squirrels, birds, mice, rabbits, and carrion, and are especially fond of porcupines. Fishers attack porcupines

with extraordinary speed and agility, slashing at the nose and head, where there are few quills. Once its prey is dead, the fisher flops it over onto its back, and proceeds to eat its way through the soft underside. The voracious animal leaves little more than bones in a pouch of skin and quills lying upon the forest floor. Curiously, the fisher seems rarely to suffer ill effects from porcupine quills, even when the barbs are driven deep into the flesh.

Between Long Lake and Round Pond, the river winds through a magnificent stand of forest. Lovely side brooks — Sweeney, Whittaker, Gamash, and Henderson — open narrow corridors to the river, inviting exploration. Here one fully senses the awesome density of woods described by Thoreau:

You may penetrate half a dozen rods farther into that twilight wilderness, after some dry bark to kindle your fire with, and wonder what mysteries lie hidden still deeper in it, say at the end of a long day's walk; or you may run down to the shore for a dipper of water and get a clearer view for a short distance up and down the stream, and while you stand there, see a fish leap, or duck alight in the river, or hear a wood thrush or robin sing in the woods. That is as if you had been to town or civilized parts. But there is no sauntering off to see the country, and ten or fifteen rods seems a great way from your companions, and you come back with the air of a much-traveled man, as from a long journey, with adventures to relate, though you may have heard the crackling of the fire all the while — and at a hundred yards you might be lost past recovery.

Elsewhere he adds: "In some of those dense fir and spruce woods there is hardly room for the smoke to go up. The trees are a standing night, and every fir and spruce which you fell is a plume plucked from night's raven wing."

The river pushes on, past Michaud Farm, and thunders over Allagash Falls, a foaming chute where the river drops some thirty feet. The end of the waterway, at Twin Brooks, is five miles from where the Allagash enters the St. John. A voyage down the entire Wilderness Waterway takes from seven to ten days and is an unforgettable experience.

205

Dawn mists rise from the surface of Moosehead Lake (above), largest of the numerous lakes and ponds in the north woods of Maine.

206–207. Allagash Stream rushes through a mixed hardwood forest of birches and balsam fir. The six-mile-long waterway, which is swift and rocky, connects the tranquil beauty of Allagash Lake with Chamberlain Lake, close to the beginning of the Allagash Wilderness Waterway.

208

The colorful leaves of
red maple and other
hardwoods are scattered
across a granite bank of
Allagash Stream while a
brimming pothole reflects
the forest above it. A
moose, for whom the
ponds and marshes of the

are owned by large
logging companies. The
Allagash Wilderness
Waterway, which was
created by the Maine
legislature in 1966,
protects only narrow
fringes of forest on either
side of the waterway from

Allagash Stream is a
shallow, lively stream,
plunging through cascades
(above left) and over Little
Allagash Falls (above and
left). Because it can be
difficult to navigate and is
an offshoot of the main
waterway, Allagash
Stream is not as frequently
visited as most of the river
system, and retains a
pristine grandeur.

Seen from a distance, conifers often seem to merge into a single homogeneous forest, yet the age and footing of these trees in the vicinity of Allagash Stream and Round Pond reveal them to be highly individualistic. The base of a pitch pine (far left) is knotty and bulbous, while the roots of a yellow pine intertwine with shards of rock (left) and those of a northern white cedar (right) seem smooth as the muscles of a man's arm.

213

214–215. *Autumn sunrise, Allagash Lake. At this time of day the calm waters usually provide an almost perfect mirror image, but as Thoreau noted: "Looking off from the shore, a surface may appear to be . . . almost smooth . . . but when you get out so far . . . a wave will gently creep up the side of the canoe and fill your lap."*

214

At left, sunset gilds a path across the darkening waters of Eagle Lake. At twilight, many species of animals which are largely quiescent during the day begin to stir. Black bear (right) prowl the shoreline, rolling over logs in search of grubs and foraging among berry bushes. Various species of frogs, including Pickering's tree frogs, bullfrogs, and leopard frogs, begin their nightly serenade. Occasionally, the lonely, haunting cry of a loon will sound across the dimness of the water.

217

A forest in the vicinity of Umsaskis Lake. With the turning of leaves in autumn, the forests of northern Maine often seem to take on the soft, subtle color mixes of an Impressionist painting. A clump of pearly everlasting (right) stands out vividly against the forest floor. Many wildflowers, including witch hazel, twinflowers, dwarf dogwood, and lady slipper—a delicate wild orchid—are found along the Allagash, as well as mushrooms such as the golden chanterelle, a gourmet's delight.

At left, a beaver nibbles quaking aspen leaves. For nearly two centuries, European gentlemen considered hats fashioned from beaver pelts to be as essential as trousers, and consequently the beaver population of the north woods was severely depleted. Fortunately, at about the time trappers and traders realized that the North American beaver population was limited, the fashion waned. Today, beaver thrive throughout northern Maine; their dams have created countless ponds. Beaver may have gnawed the spruce tree at right with the intention of using it as a dam or for the food value of its soft underbark.

222–223. Foam beneath Allagash Falls constantly swirls into shifting abstract patterns. The falls, close to the end of the Wilderness Waterway, drops more than thirty feet through a foaming chute. This was the only major obstacle to log drives on the river in the early days of logging in this area.

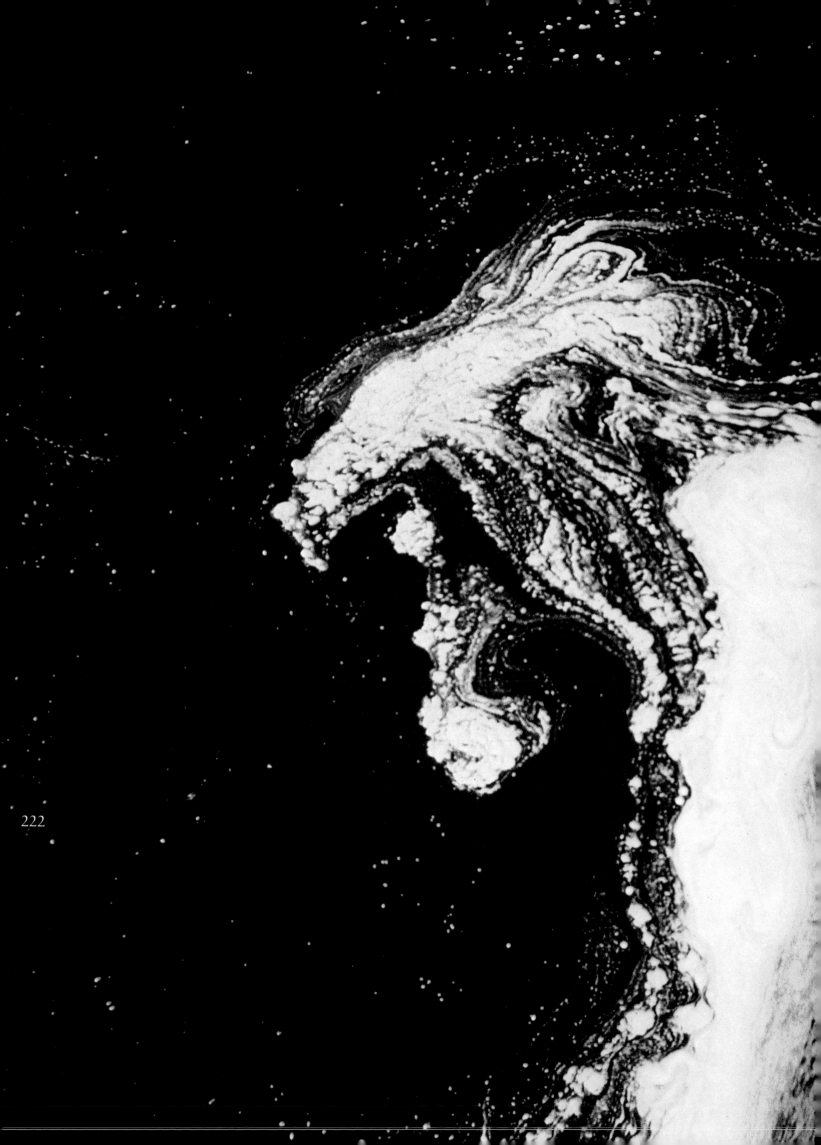

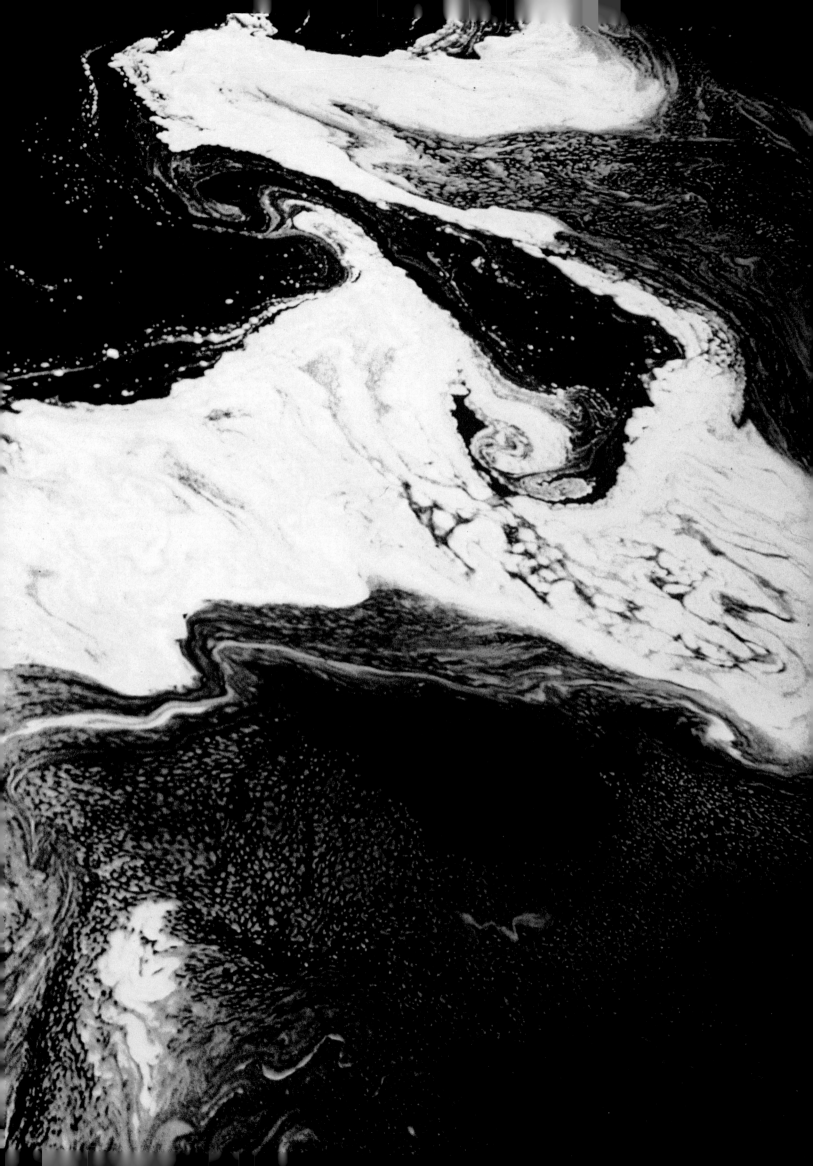

The Allagash River,
its volume swollen
by the contributions of
numerous clear streams,
surges through the forest
below Allagash Falls.
Scotch-Irish settlers began
to move into the country
around this lower section
of the river in the
mid-1830's—most of them
earning a meagre living by
both farming and logging.

Details of riverine life
on the Allagash River.
As with all wilderness
rivers, minute details are
often more interesting
than dramatic shapes.
Floating maple leaves
(below) throw bold
shadows. Tree trunks
(right) are reflected in a
pond, and few elements of
nature are more graceful
than the flanks of eastern
brook trout (bottom).

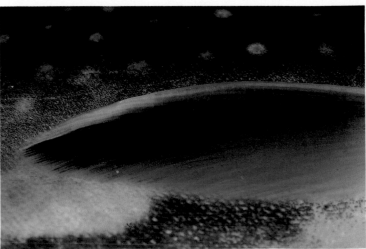

228–229. *The Allagash River, here seen between Allagash Falls and Allagash village, swings past boulders deposited by the last ice age. Only about ten thousand years ago, retreating glaciers left a granite shield which was scraped and gouged. Thousands of lakes and ponds were created as debris dammed the folds and basins.*

230–231. *Autumn haze softens the outlines of hills above the Allagash River as it approaches its confluence with the St. John River. Both rivers wind through forested, semi-wilderness areas until they merge and enter a populated farming valley.*

228

230

Photographs by Dan Budnik

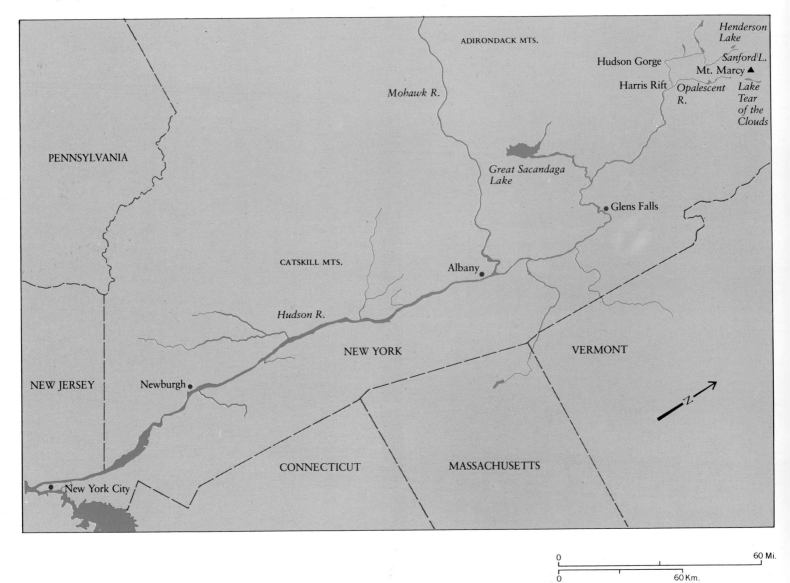

ADIRONDACK MTS.

Henderson Lake

Hudson Gorge

Sanford L.

Mt. Marcy ▲

Harris Rift

Mohawk R.

Opalescent R.

Lake Tear of the Clouds

PENNSYLVANIA

Great Sacandaga Lake

• Glens Falls

CATSKILL MTS.

Albany •

Hudson R.

NEW YORK

VERMONT

NEW JERSEY

Newburgh •

CONNECTICUT

MASSACHUSETTS

-z-

• New York City

0   60 Mi.

0   60 Km.

The Upper Hudson

Three hundred and fifteen miles from where New York Harbor, one of the busiest places on earth, opens into the Atlantic Ocean, the Hudson River begins as a quiet tarn cupped by three of the highest peaks in the Adirondack Mountains. The shallow brook which slips away from it is soon joined by other swift streams, and by the time these waters flow under the highway bridge at the village of Newcomb, a fair-sized mountain river has been formed. It tumbles its way between thick stands of spruce, balsam fir, and mountain ash, making abrupt bends where it has carved its channel along ancient rock faults. Much of the upper river is accessible only by boat or by hiking through the dense foliage on its banks. Black bear weighing as much as six hundred pounds prowl the mountains looming above the river. Deer drink water at eddies where trout slip past in quick pursuit of flies that land upon the surface of the water.

Near Glens Falls the river emerges from the mountains and becomes tamer. Many of the farms in this country are roughhewn and weathered. Their chicken coops and duck ponds are periodically raided by freebooters from the mountain forest — red foxes, raccoons, and skunks. The rushing adolescence of the river quickly matures and it becomes deeper, straighter, flanked by roads and a railroad. Paper mills and other industrial plants begin to dominate its banks. A few years ago their discharge of pollutants was so wanton that scientists predicted the eventual destruction of much of the aquatic life of the river. Since then, tougher controls on the handling of waste materials from industry and riverbank communities has begun to reverse the change.

At Troy, although barely out of the mountains of its birth and still 150 miles from the open Atlantic, the Hudson becomes a tidal estuary and accommodates seagoing vessels. As the river passes in the shadow of the legendary Catskills and slices between the Hudson Highlands, it still appears to be a proper river rather than a fiord; yet by Newburgh the water has become slightly saline. But spring runoff sends such a surge of snowmelt into the Hudson that the ocean's thrust may be pushed back as far south as Yonkers. Marine species of fish — striped bass, blueback herring, shad, and sturgeon — move upriver to spawn. Algae grows rapidly in the warm shallow sections such as the Tappan Zee, off Tarrytown, twenty miles north of New York City, nourishing the microscopic animals that provide food for fish larvae and fingerlings, which in turn are eaten by larger fish.

The deep, glacially gouged channel of the lower Hudson cuts past the Catskills, the pushed-up folds of an ancient semitropical sea where even today one finds the outlines of starfish, corals, and sea lilies in eroded gullies. It was back in these high hills, named for the wildcats which still inhabit them, where Washington Irving imagined Rip Van Winkle sleeping for twenty years after a monumental spree with some gnomes whose bowling set up peals of thunder. When Henry Hudson sailed up these waters in 1609, Indians invited

233

him into a circular dwelling of oak bark, where they served him wild pigeon and presented him with otter pelts.

After being squeezed into a tight channel by mountains — Storm King, Bear, Dunderberg, and High Tor — the Hudson broadens into Haverstraw Bay and Tappan Zee before passing the basaltic wall of the Palisades and entering the bustle of New York Harbor.

Mt. Marcy, highest mountain in New York State, was ancient long before the Rockies or the Alps had started to push upward. Some of its rocks are a billion years old. Algonquin Indians called it Tahawas — the cloud splitter. A little more than a thousand feet below its bald summit, a pond marks the headwaters of the Hudson River. In 1872, Verplanck Colvin, official surveyor for the state of New York, came upon the small body of water while making a topographic study of the Adirondacks. His official report to the New York State legislature reflected his excitement: "Far above the chilly waters of Lake Avalanche, at an elevation of 4,293 feet [since adjusted to 4,322]...is a minute, unpretending tear of the clouds...a lively pool shivering in the breezes of the mountains, and sending its limpid surplus through Feldspar Brook and to the Opalescent River, the wellspring of the Hudson." Sharing Colvin's enthusiasm, the legislators decided to officially name the pool Lake Tear of the Clouds.

There are other sources of the Hudson, such as lovely and lonely Elk Lake, but Lake Tear of the Clouds is the highest. This two-acre sheet of water, with marsh grasses at one end and a rim of spruce and fir around the rest of it, seems a long way indeed from the Hudson at Manhattan, as does moss-lined Feldspar Brook, over which deer can easily bound. The evergreens are stunted at this elevation, and are rarely more than thirty feet high.

Feldspar Brook drops rapidly through the narrow cleft it has carved in hard ancient rock; it is too swift and cold to support any fish except perhaps sculpins or darters. It soon joins the Opalescent River, which spills over fifty-foot falls, lingers in narrow green pools, and slides over gravel beds in which chips of hornblende, feldspar, and mica glisten. Here the dominance of evergreens has given way to a forest which includes birches, oaks, maple, and hickory. Below Henderson Lake — scarcely seven miles from Lake Tear of the Clouds — the source waters have tumbled down almost two thirds of their vertical descent to sea level.

Iron ore was discovered on Henderson Lake in 1826, but another decade passed before the wilderness above the lake was explored. Geologists Ebenezer Emmons and James Hall bushwhacked their way up the Opalescent River in 1836, finally arriving at a small, high body of water which they named Lake Colden. This, they believed, was the source of the Hudson, having failed to trace Feldspar Brook to Lake Tear of the Clouds. Although the true source of the river remained undiscovered for another thirty-six years, their report was valuable for its descriptions of the wild nature of the country at that time. They saw numerous deer and moose tracks. Once, breaking suddenly into a clearing, they surprised two wolves which were feeding upon a deer carcass. A mountain lion seriously mauled their dog.

This kind of isolation would not last for long. Hunters soon began to prowl the streams which feed into the upper Hudson and the slopes above them. By 1861 the last moose had been killed. Today, there are no longer any wolves or mountain lions. So many beaver were trapped that by the winter of 1894–95 only a handful remained; before the species became totally extinct, trapping was finally prohibited, and the animals have made a dramatic comeback. Whitetail deer, once slaughtered by market hunters, have also returned in numbers. Today, the deer population of Essex County, which contains the headwaters of the Hudson, exceeds the human population.

A rocky shallow stream some twenty feet wide emerges from Henderson Lake. It is the Hudson River, subject to the ravages of civilization almost from the start: A wall of black slag a hundred feet high looms above it, waste from a titanium mine. The mine is an old one, and a huge semicircular gash has been torn into the rock. On working days smoke curls up from the mine stacks. A rubble of processed rock follows the valley for almost a mile. For most of the remaining miles to Harris Lake the river is usually within a stone's throw of a road, railroad, or both.

Once the river leaves the lake, swirling beneath the bridge of State Highway 28N, it plunges into wild, unoccupied country. For twenty-one miles it runs far from roads or settlements. As it works its way down through the mountains, the river is generally swift, bucking between and over boulders. Yet on some stretches, such as Blackwell Stillwater, the current slows and the forest draws back from marsh grasses and meadows containing bunchberry, large-leafed goldenrod, and wood sorrel. One can move gently across the water, watching the banks and sky for wildlife. Magnificent blue and white goshawks glide above the river, keen eyes searching for mice, red squirrels, and grouse. The supple river otter may pause in their quest for crayfish, berries, and minnows to slide gleefully down a mud slick, not just once, but again and again. The cubs of the black bear, common along the upper Hudson, are also sportive. I once saw a young cub, scarcely bigger than a leather medicine ball, tuck itself into a round position and roll down a steep grassy incline. Its twin followed as the mother, who was not aware of me, watched protectively from the rim of the bank.

The black bear population appears to be increasing along the upper Hudson, but the otter live a more precarious existence. Although common throughout most of the United States half a century ago, the otter is now extinct in many of its former haunts, and diminishing rapidly in others. Ironically, their decline is at least partially due to the writing of two men whose overall effect upon wildlife conservation has been beneficial. Both Izaac Walton and Ernest Thompson Seton denounced otters for consuming great quantities of trout, salmon, and other game fish. Zealous anglers continued to kill or trap otter illegally in spite of the fact that zoologists now find that fish make up only a third of the otter's diet, and that they are far more likely to feed upon sticklebacks, minnows, suckers, and sculpins than game fish, which are faster and harder to catch.

During the spring runoff, Harris Rift becomes a wild toss of whitewater over the boulder-strewn channel of the river. The most violent stretch is a 200-yard-long chute known as Big Nasty Rapids. In the past, when timber was annually floated down the river during runoff, several loggers drowned here. From time to time canoes are demolished in Big Nasty, but their occupants, buoyed by life preservers, usually manage to crawl ashore suffering little more than chill and perhaps a bruise or two.

Over the years, a number of artists have been drawn to this dramatic stretch of the river. During the 1880s, Winslow Homer was a frequent visitor. Although he was fond of remarking that he came to the country of the upper Hudson to fish for trout and get away from his work, some of his finest watercolors — *Casting in the Falls, Leaping Trout, Boy Fishing,* and *Mink Pond* — were painted here.

At the confluence of the Indian River the Hudson swings abruptly to the east, narrows, and begins to drop into steepwalled Hudson Gorge. In late afternoon this is a shadowy rift of rushing water; even the names of nearby features add an aura of mystery — Bad Luck Mountain, O K Slip Brook, P Gay Mountain. Pine Mountain rises sharply for a thousand feet above Harris Rift. After breaking out of the Hudson Gorge into the gentler valley of the Boreas River, the Hudson emerges from the back country at the village of North River.

North River was a logging town in the days when logs were skidded to the water, branded with a company sign, and then shoved downstream. The bark was left on the logs so that lumberjacks wearing cog soles could get a purchase on them as they jockeyed timber in the water. A good riverman could spin and work the logs with assurance. Yet, fine loggers were occasionally drowned. They were an individualistic breed. One man insisted his bunk lie parallel to the river flow, and when a chore boy tried to shift his bed "cross current" he changed it back. In their idle hours the loggers of the upper Hudson River often amused themselves with songs or tall stories.

Adirondack guides of the period were generally hardy, resourceful, and salty as well as good yarnspinners. They developed the design of the Adirondack guide boat, which combined the best qualities of the canoe and the rowboat. Several thousand brass screws and copper nails joined the pine or cedar planking of these sturdy sixteen-foot vessels, yet they were light enough to be easily portaged.

Charles Warner, a friend of Mark Twain and a great admirer of the Adirondack guides, was bemused by their lack of interest in personal hygiene. He quoted one of them as saying that he never took baths because "I don't believe in that eternal sozzlin!" In describing this guide, Warner observed that: "His clothes seemed to have been put on him once for all, like the bark of a tree, a long time ago."

On September 14, 1901, Vice President Theodore Roosevelt was hailed by a messenger at Lake Tear of the Clouds as he was descending from the summit of Mt. Marcy. He was informed that President William McKinley, who had been wounded by an anarchist eight days previously, had suffered a relapse. Roosevelt and his party hurried down the mountain to the Tahawas Lodge, arriving after dark. His secretary called to say he had a waiting locomotive with full steam up at North Creek, forty miles away over rough mountain wagon roads. Roosevelt and his driver set off in a buckboard. It was raining, slippery, and so dark that the driver could barely see his horses — yet the Vice President insisted they careen full speed through the night. At one point, skimming the edge of a cliff, the driver suggested they slow down. Roosevelt said: "Not at all. Push ahead." It was dawn when the buckboard was reined up in front of the North Creek station, and Roosevelt learned that he was now President. McKinley had died during the night.

The historic station where Roosevelt was sworn in is now the site of another event — the starting point of the annual Hudson River White Water Derby. By early May the river is gorged with the snow water of dozens of creeks and brooks, and the current pounds its way over boulders. The Derby started modestly enough in 1958 with 24 entries. Most of the spectators were either families of the contestants or people from nearby river villages. Today the Derby draws over 600 entries and some 15,000 enthusiasts mill about in the streets of North Creek and Riparius. They listen to bluegrass music and crowd the banks of the river. Families picnic while, bundled in blankets, young couples practice other rites of spring.

There is a day of slalom races, patterned after the ski event. Here, canoeists attempt to pass through a series of aluminum "gates" without touching them. Since many of the gates are in the wildest churns of white-water, the aim is not only to make it through the gate, but to avoid capsizing. A good many contestants end up in the water.

The second day of the Derby features a downriver race from North Creek to Riparius. Between these two towns the river bows out away from the highway, and rushes through a thick forest of hardwoods and evergreens. This is one of the most beautiful sections of the river.

Beyond Riparius, the Hudson continues to wander the back country, breaking into haphazard waves as it charges through the Horse Race, idling around forested points where, in season, blossoms of goldthread, bunchberry, trillium, enchanter's nightshade, star flower, and Indian pine flaunt their extravagant colors. By day there are always at least two sounds, those of birds and water moving. As one drifts quietly, the sky may be filled with the clear song of a single thrush; or at twilight one may hear the excited cries of many birds as they mob an owl. Mobbing is one of the most curious of all bird activities. If one of the small birds upon which owls sometimes prey discovers an owl, sharp calls may bring dozens of other birds of various species, all clamoring over the discovery of an enemy. The owl, depending upon stealth, thus has no chance of surprising a victim. Days or even weeks after the owl has left the vicinity, small birds will sometimes return to the spot where it was initially sighted, and wheel and cry as if it were still there.

The other sound, that of water, is a complexity of rhythms ranging from the full roar of spring flood thrusting its power over and between mid-river boulders to the whispers of an eddy brushing sand and grass. Drifting off to sleep beside a lonely campfire on the upper river, the Hudson of Manhattan with its raw and ceaseless human energy translated through light and sound seems incalculably distant.

Beyond Thurman Station, the Hudson begins to gentle out; grazing pastures stretch from its banks and farms appear with increasing frequency. At Glens Falls, the Hudson becomes a river of settlement, history, and commerce. Yet between Lake Tear of the Clouds and Glens Falls the music of wild mountain water still plays, and, one hopes, forever will.

237–239. *Close to the summit of Mt. Marcy, a large boulder perches on a shoulder of ancient, scarred rock. About a million years ago during the Pleistocene epoch, vast ice sheets covered the Adirondacks. Some 10,000 years ago the last glaciers retreated, leaving slopes scoured to billion-year-old bedrock and numerous glacial erratics and shaped rocks carried by the ponderous frozen flows. Mt. Marcy (overleaf, center foreground), reaching 5,344 feet, is the highest peak in the Adirondacks.*

238

240

The Hudson River begins at Lake Tear of the Clouds, a quiet tarn a little more than a thousand feet below the summit of Mt. Marcy. Although there are other sources of the Hudson, such as lonely Elk Lake, Lake Tear of the Clouds is the highest. While Lake Tear of the Clouds is only 315 miles from the bustle of New York Harbor, it was not recognized as the headwaters of the river until surveyor Verplanck Colvin came upon it in 1872.

242–243. *Fed by the melting snow of early summer, Feldspar Brook rushes past mossy boulders. Lake Tear of the Clouds drains into Feldspar Brook, which drops rapidly through chutes it has carved in hard, ancient rock.*

244–245. *Clouds linger in the valley behind Lake Colden, created when debris from retreating glaciers blocked a stream. The two geologists who discovered the lake in 1836 assumed it to be the source of the Hudson, having failed to trace Feldspar Brook to Lake Tear of the Clouds.*

The Opalescent River (below) flows beneath trees toppled by a hurricane which raked across the Adirondacks in 1950. Lake Colden is the source of the Opalescent River, which was named for the chips of hornblende, feldspar, and mica which glisten in the gravels of its bed.

Calamity Brook (left), another Hudson River headwater stream, tumbles down a mountain slope. Although the river accommodates ocean-going vessels for almost half of its length, it begins as a series of swift, shallow waterways in the highlands of Adirondack Park, a semi-wilderness region larger than the state of Massachusetts.

Feldspar Brook (above) joins the Opalescent River. The first party to push through the wild country to Lake Colden saw deer and moose tracks and surprised two wolves feeding upon a deer carcass. A mountain lion mauled one of their dogs. Moose, mountain lion, and wolves are no longer found in the region, but white-tail deer flourish.

Below, an afternoon breeze stirs the surface of Henderson Lake into intricate patterns. Although iron ore was discovered beside Henderson Lake in 1826, it was not until the 1870's that the lake, as well as the surrounding mountains, became popular with anglers and hikers.

Grasses and shoreline ripples form an abstract design at Henderson Lake (bottom). The upper Hudson River and high peaks of the Adirondacks provided inspiration for a number of painters, including Winslow Homer.

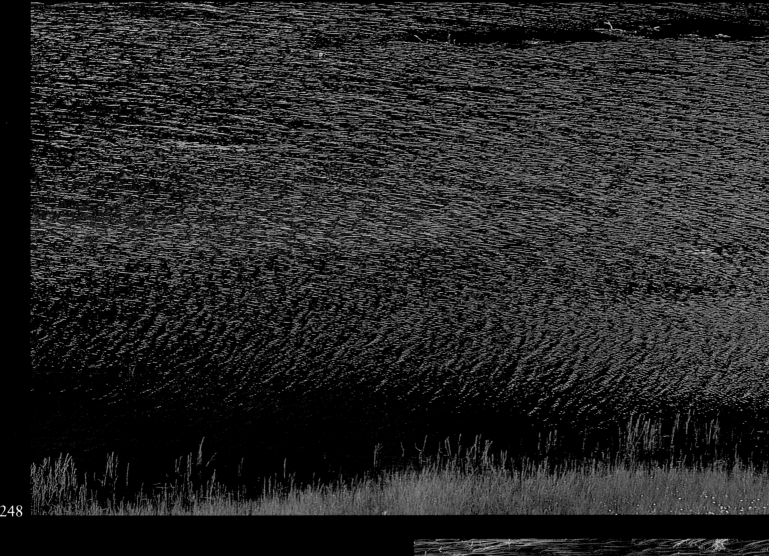

248

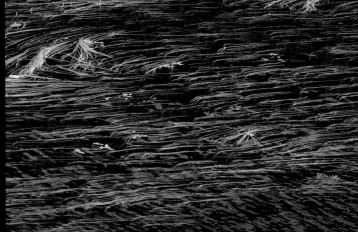

The Hudson is still no
more than a brook as
it enters the upper end of
Sanford Lake (below). Two
white-tailed deer freeze,
half-concealed in the
protection of a thicket.
There are more deer in
Essex County, which
contains the Hudson River
headwaters, than there are
humans.

250–251. *A becalmed
Henderson Lake.
Calamity Brook flows into
the upper end of the mile-
long lake; the Hudson
River, here a twenty-foot-
wide brook, rushes out of
it. Although only seven
miles in a bee line from
Lake Tear of the Clouds,
the Hudson source waters
have tumbled down
almost two-thirds of their
vertical descent to sea level.*

250

The Hudson (below), gathering strength from numerous fast, chill tributaries, surges through a forest of mixed hardwoods below Blue Ledges. In the distance, mist rises into the chill air of early morning from the warmer moving current.

At right, the Hudson River loops its way through the densely forested slopes of the Hudson Gorge. For 21 miles, from Harris Lake to the village of North River, the Hudson flows through wild, unoccupied country.

252

254–255. *In Harris Rift, the wildest stretch of the upper Hudson, a series of boulder-strewn rapids create a chaos of savage crosscurrents, breaking waves, and deep holes.*

Photographs by Wendell Metzen

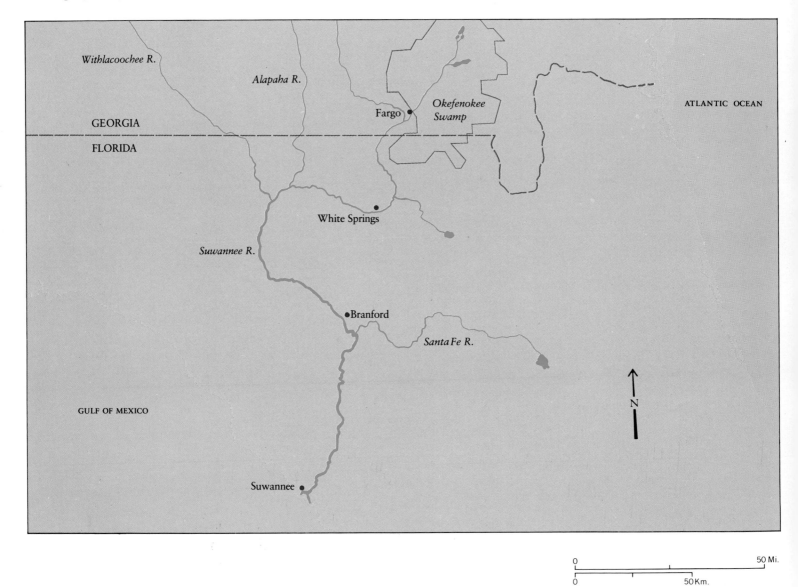

Withlacoochee R.

Alapaha R.

GEORGIA

Fargo

Okefenokee Swamp

ATLANTIC OCEAN

FLORIDA

White Springs

Suwannee R.

Branford

Santa Fe R.

GULF OF MEXICO

N

Suwannee

0   50 Mi.

0   50 Km.

The Suwannee

The Suwannee River begins as gentle, almost imperceptible currents drifting through the Okefenokee Swamp of southeastern Georgia. At the edge of the swamp, leisurely strands of tea-colored water converge into a slow, crooked flow which passes between sandbanks and limestone cliffs. There are only a few scattered towns along the river. For much of its 265-mile length it splits dense, moss-hung forests which seem as wild and unfrequented as when sixteenth-century Spanish explorers floundered through them in quest of gold.

Most of us have been introduced to the Suwannee by Stephen Foster's ballad "Old Folks at Home." When the composer wrote the lines "Way down upon the Swannee River, far, far away..." he had never been nearer than several hundred miles from the river. But he chanced upon the name in an atlas, changed the spelling, and instantly immortalized it.

Most of the Suwannee's headwaters, the 640-square-mile Okefenokee Swamp, is a federal wildlife refuge. It is a curious, illusionary place, neither lake nor land, but a hauntingly beautiful combination of both. There are vast prairies of green and flowering vegetation which seem solid enough to hike across. Yet the tightly bunched sedges, pickerelweed, lily pads, and floating hearts are actually covering water one to four feet deep.

Much of the Okefenokee is thickly forested with cypress, gum, and slash pine. Although some of the stands are rooted in the sandy soil of islands, others rise directly from shallow water or spongy "houses," domes of peat which have been bulged to the surface by marsh gas. More than one lost traveler, seeing a rim of trees in the distance and assuming that he was approaching the edge of the swamp or an island, has canoed to within a stone's throw of the trees before realizing that his forest is little more than a slender row of partially submerged cypress, as insubstantial as a stage set.

Major-General G.A. McCall, an observant wanderer, remarked upon another curious aspect of the swamp in his *Letters from the Frontier,* which was published in 1868:

As the sun rose the following morning... I looked out upon the lake, when, to my no little surprise, the island I had observed the previous day had disappeared, and on further examination the water of the lake seemed to have receded from the shore nearly one hundred yards. It was not until I had walked down to the shore of the lake that I discovered that the island I had discovered the day before had drifted with the wind against the shore where I stood.

Such floating islets of muck often support a surprising amount of vegetation and even small trees. They undulate when a man walks on them, causing brush and trees to sway — hence the name Okefenokee, which comes from Indian words meaning "trembling earth."

257

Indians and swampers — the pioneer settlers who drifted into the region from the Appalachian Mountains— poled canoes or shallow-draft *bateaux* through the swamp on an intricate network of runs. These narrow, open channels wind through the thick vegetation of the prairies and into the twilight depths of the forest. In some places the runs open into ponds or narrow lakes where the surface of the water, because of the dark peat beneath it, renders an almost perfect mirror image. Clouds, overhanging mossy trees, and the flap of an occasional bird all seem to be passing beneath the bow of one's canoe.

Roughly a half million to a million years ago the Oke-fenokee was a shallow ocean bay. Over the centuries a 100-mile-long sandbar turned the bay into a lagoon and finally sealed it off from the sea altogether. As rain and the sluggish flow of creeks gradually flushed away the salt water, aquatic plants flourished. They decayed to form thickening beds of peat, which rose close enough to the surface so that sedges and other marsh plants could take root. These, in turn, provided hum-mocks of decayed vegetation and soil from which trees would later grow.

Camp Cornelia, seven miles southwest of Folkston, Georgia, on the edge of the swamp, is a small store where one can rent canoes and buy fishing tackle and picnic items. This is the beginning of the Suwannee Canal, a monumental fiasco. During the two decades after the Civil War, the Okefenokee was inhabited only by a scattering of self-reliant swampers who trapped, fished, and hunted along its runs. Captain Harry Jack-son, a wealthy resident of Atlanta, had noted the valuable stands of cypress in the swamp and determined to build a series of canals to drain it. There would then be easy access to the timber, he reasoned, and the exposed land, given a little time to dry out, could be sold to farmers as pasture. His Suwannee Canal Company pur-chased the Okefenokee from the state of Georgia for fourteen and a half cents per acre in 1889. Although 22 miles of canal were dredged out at considerable expense, the swamp remained obdurately swamplike, and the project was abandoned at Jackson's death four years later.

On the low, muddy banks of the canal, alligators like 258 to sun themselves, watching the passing boats and canoes with a heavy-lidded indolence, their jaws some-times agape as if considering the boatmen as possible prey. Although there is no record of anyone having been seriously injured by an alligator in the Suwannee refuge, there have been incidents. A game officer once stepped out of his skiff onto what he took to be a log. The "log" suddenly shifted, the ranger lost his balance, and a huge warty head swung around to take a nip out of his rump.

A canoe trail branches off from the Suwannee Canal at Mizell Prairie — a three-foot-wide crack in a green expanse of water plants. The canoe trails, maintained by the refuge staff, follow the natural runs wherever possible. Signposts thrusting out of the water, spaced a mile apart, indicate distances to a given place or announce a turn. Between the signs, white-tipped poles show the way. In a world where a canoeist paddles through nearly impenetrable, half-drowned forests and acres of floating flowers where runs are constantly opening and closing, the trail markers are no guarantee against getting lost, as I have done. But they help. The prairies are host to a variety of waterfowl — several species of ducks, cranes, herons, and egrets. The egrets possess an ambassadorial dignity, standing quietly in the water amid lily pads and iris blossoms. If you approach too closely, they flap away with fluid, languid grace.

Beyond the open reaches of Mizell and then Chase Prairie, the canoe trail approaches Floyd's Island through a forest of cypress and blackgum where the leaves interlock overhead. Paddling through this dim, twisting tunnel, I once heard a large animal crashing and splashing through the thick foliage and shallow water off to one side. It was probably a black bear. Their thick hides allow them to get through brush so thick it would take the skin off a lean man. They seem so comfortable with the wetness of the swamp that one old-timer used to declare he was sure they could walk across the water. It may, of course, have been one of the legendary and elusive Piney Ridge Rooters of the swamp — domesticated pigs which have run wild for so long that their bristles are said to be as tough as porcupine quills. Back among the maple trees of Floyd's Island is a deserted hunting lodge which was built by a timber baron.

There never was much logging on Floyd's Island, but in 1908 the Hebard Lumber Company ran thirty-five miles of railroad over pilings to nearby Billy's Island. There was soon a logging camp of 600 people, and huge cypress, some of them over 300 years old, began to fall. Most of the swampers were of such solitary persuasion that they regarded the logging operation on Billy's Island as akin to an urban invasion. Fortunately for those of us who share the swampers' proclivity to solitude, the Hebard operation shut down in 1927.

The canoe trail between Floyd's Island and Bluff Lake twists through a thick forest, where tree branches and vines mingle overhead, diffusing the sunlight. In certain places bulges of peat moss make paddling impossible. One uses the paddles for poling as well as for sweeping gaps in the cobwebs that occasionally all but veil the narrow passage. Here one is at the very heart of the swamp, surrounded by vegetation and the pungent smells of growth and decay. There are butterflies of every color of the spectrum. Turtles and frogs slip off mossy logs.

One afternoon a friend and I took a wrong turn and had to backtrack for three miles. Since there is little dry land in this section of the Okefenokee, we began to paddle hard, hoping to reach Bluff Lake by nightfall. At Bluff Lake, as at other places along the canoe trails, shelters have been erected on pilings to accommodate overnight campers. Thunderheads had been boiling up all afternoon. Shortly after dusk the storm exploded. Sheets of lightning were dramatically reflected in the open patches of water we were now crossing. A cardinal rule of boating is to get off of the water during a thunderstorm — yet here we were surrounded by miles of it. By the time the full force of the rain hit us, we had entered a thick grove of blackgum and cypress trees. They sheltered us, after a fashion, but they also obscured the light; there was no way we could continue on to Bluff Lake in darkness.

Bivouacking in an overloaded canoe is a unique experience, especially in the middle of a swamp. Unknown animals splashed close to the canoe; others made sounds in branches overhead. Off in the blackness an owl screeched. Frogs were piping, croaking, and humming all over the place. There are over twenty species of frogs in the Okefenokee, including such exotics as the bronze, barking treefrog, eastern narrowmouth, ornate chorus, and southern leopard. One small green fellow with protruding yellow eyes squatted upon a lily pad a few inches from the canoe, maintaining his vigil until it was nearly dawn.

From Bluff Lake the most frequented canoe trail skirts the swamp at Kingfisher Landing and then winds back into the center of the Okefenokee. The trail, often following leads which have been used by Indians, trappers, and moonshiners, burrows its way beneath towering stands of cypress and gum. In some spots during the spring, the thick blanket of leaves makes a twilight at high noon. Certain mudbanks are so scored and cross-hatched by the feet of numerous birds, raccoons, opossums, and other creatures that they resemble panels of Egyptian hieroglyphics.

The two campsites along this trail, at Maul Hammock Lake and Big Water Lake, are plank platforms built over the water, as at Bluff Lake. It is a strange experience to waken in the middle of the night and hear a fish jumping beneath your sleeping bag. And the fish do jump. Big Water Lake, despite the name, is a pond less than half a mile long and about thirty feet wide. Yet back in 1925, before limits were imposed upon fishing, forty thousand warmouth, catfish, jackfish and largemouth bass were taken from this scrap of water. Their descendants still thrive, nourished by the rich food chains of the swamp.

The canoe trail ends at the roadhead on the western side of the Stephen C. Foster State Park. The Suwannee River leaves the Okefenokee near this campground. The upper Suwannee pushes through a transitional region where in times of sustained rainfall shallow sheets of water stretch for miles in every direction. The groves of stunted tupelos as well as solitary cypresses are filled with snakes, rodents, and other creatures that normally do much of their foraging upon dry land. Alligators roar in the night. Yet during a drought the river threads through basins of cracked mud, and the hammering bill of a pileated woodpecker or the scurry of ants rushing about to consolidate newly acquired empires seem to be the only signs of life.

Beyond Fargo, the Suwannee cuts through sand hills covered with scrub pine and oak and then swings in long, lazy loops through magnificent forests of live oak and red bay. The river water has a slightly rusty cast to it — the stain of tannic acid leached from decaying bark and leaves — and the beaches have an oddly ashen color. Drifting beneath Spanish moss dangling from limbs, one has a sense of nostalgic Southern Gothic even before reaching the first faded ante-bellum mansions at White Springs. A little above White Springs the drowsy river suddenly comes to life and drops more than eight feet over a brace of limestone ledges. All of this is limestone country. The ground is veined throughout with the soluble rock, honeycombed with subterranean channels of water. Numerous springs pulse out of the limestone, sometimes clear, sometimes mineral-laden.

Before they were driven out of northern Florida to take refuge in the Everglades, Seminole Indians often trekked to White Springs to bathe in its mineral waters. Later, ornate hotels rose above the ashes of their camp-fires, and ladies with upswept hair, bustles, and para-sols wandered among the flowers of meticulously groomed gardens. When I passed through White Springs a few years back, a couple of these once-proud hotels — now deserted, warped ghosts — rose from a rabble of natural growth.

Beyond White Springs the river, still looping around as if determined never to reach the sea, continues to wash through cypress groves whose mossy branches often meet overhead. Stretching away from the banks, grassy pastures dotted with cattle can be seen with increasing frequency. With the influx of the Alapaha and Withla-coochee rivers, as well as the crystal flows forced out of four sizable springs — Clear, Blue, Bluff, and Troy — the Suwannee begins to broaden and take on volume.

There are still narrow channels with overhanging trees, however, as well as shoals and mudbars. When a flamboyant early-day steamboat captain, James Tucker, announced his intention to run his paddlewheeler, the *Madison*, upriver from Branford to White Springs, other river pilots were skeptical. Impossible, they declared. Captain Tucker replied that he would make the voyage even if he lost his boat's superstructure in doing it. He all but did. The *Madison* finally arrived at

White Springs with paddles splintered, superstructure battered, and both smokestacks and pilot cabin torn away by overhanging limbs. As relaxed and affable as if he had just made a lazy afternoon's run, Captain Tucker strolled ashore to greet the incredulous locals: he had made it.

The 110-mile run between Branford and Cedar Key, close to the mouth of the Suwannee, was once alive with steamboat traffic. Between 1886 and 1914 some thirty paddle-wheelers plied the Suwannee, bearing passengers and cargoes of peanuts, tobacco, lumber, beans, cotton, smoked hams, and other plantation products. Some of the steamboats were 200 feet long with twin stacks and double decks.

A number of plantations were scattered along the river. Perhaps some of the slaves who worked them, as Stephen Foster assumed, felt ties to the old plantation, but others ran away to join the back-country colony of a statuesque Ethiopian who called himself King Nero. Descendants of these free spirits still live far removed from the river in groves of cypress and palmettos where wild orchids flourish.

The Santa Fe River, a major tributary, joins the Suwannee below Branford. The river channel broadens from 150 to 300 yards wide. Clumps of hyacinth and quaking maiden cane drift down with the current. In the early morning and evening the surface of the river is often warmer than the air, and thick, eerie mists rise from the water. Springs continue to pulse into the Suwannee. Hart Springs is one of the largest of these, discharging fifty million gallons of water a day into the river. In the warm depths of the spring — the water remains at a constant 72 degrees. Near Old Town, a one-time steamboat tie-up, the stern-wheeler *City of Hawkinsville* sank in 1923, ending the riverboat era of the river.

As we approach the Gulf of Mexico, the river's banks broaden into swamp. Alligators, still and gray as if cast in concrete, sprawl upon mudbanks. Small green frogs plop into the water from lily pads. Sloughs trail off into expanses of water lilies and wild rice where ibises, cranes, herons, and egrets stand motionless, perhaps waiting for something or listening to a sound too faint for our ears. It is as though we had finished where we began.

The hues of sunrise (above) wash through moss-hung pond cypress lining Chesser Prairie in the Okefenokee Swamp of southeastern Georgia. The 640-square-mile swamp contains not only vast, partially submerged forests, but several open prairies where tightly bunched flowering vegetation covers wide shallow lakes.

262–263. A canoe trail threads through the floating vegetation and forested hummocks of Chase Prairie in the Okefenokee Swamp, headwaters of the Suwannee River. Sedges, pickerelweed, lily pads, floating hearts, and other aquatic plants cover the prairies so thickly that they seem to be growing from solid ground.

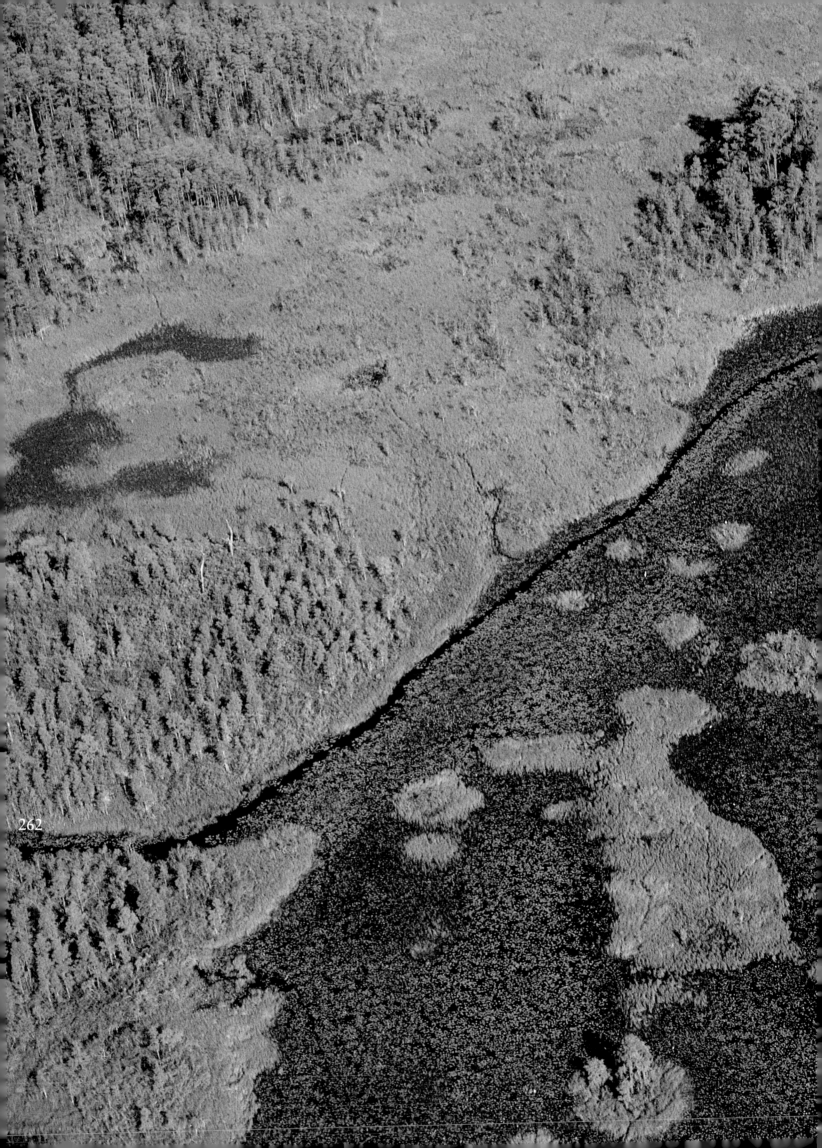

262

Golden clubs (left), semi-aquatic plants, gleaming from the surface of Chesser Prairie, are one of the more colorful plants of the Okefenokee. Pioneer trappers and alligator hunters poled shallow-draft bateaux along natural, open channels, called runs, wherever possible, and often had to cut paths through the floating plants.

Pond cypress and Neverwet plants (below) are reflected in the waters of Middle Fork Run near Billy's Lake. Although slow, almost imperceptible currents throughout the Okefenokee contribute to the Suwannee River, the main flow of the river leaves the swamp a few miles to the southwest of Billy's Lake.

Two fledgling great egrets (right) await the return of their parents to their nest, where the older birds will regurgitate small fish, frogs, and crustaceans into the beaks of their hungry offspring. Plume-hunters all but exterminated the elegant birds before the turn of the century, but the egrets have since made a dramatic comeback in places like the Okefenokee, which is now a wildlife sanctuary.

A white-tailed deer (left) drinks at the edge of the Suwannee River at Suwannee River State Park near Live Oak, Florida. The water has been stained the color of tea by tannic acid leached from decayed vegetable matter. The porous limestone banks are typical of much of the Suwannee, which receives clear water from springs.

A white ibis (above right) squabbles with a neighbor in the topmost branches of a cypress tree. Such territorial dispute, by which the birds establish and defend nesting areas, are common during the spring when hundreds of ibis may occupy the same rookery.

A limpkin (above) picks its way along a bank of the Suwannee River, searching for freshwater snails. For much of the Suwannee's 265-mile length, the river penetrates a moss-hung semi-wild forest which provides habitat for a great variety of wildlife.

The opened shell of a freshwater clam (left) lies at the edge of the river. The shell was probably left by a raccoon, who relishes the tough, hard-to-open mollusks. In places, one finds mounds of clamshells, remnants of Seminole Indian feasts before white settlement in the area.

At right, an American alligator glides across the water. After mating, females lay from forty to sixty eggs in mounds of grass and mud. Young alligators grow about a foot per year for the first six years of their lives before growth becomes more gradual. Twelve-foot alligators, with an estimated age of more than sixty years, are not uncommon.

270–271. Water lilies flaunt their brilliant petals against dark swamp water in the vicinity of the Suwannee River Delta. The American water lily, an ancient plant, is related to the lotus.

270

Notes from the Photographers

Sam Abell: The Noatak

Sam Abell's father taught him photography at home in Sylvania, Ohio. At the University of Kentucky, he worked on publications. In 1970 he became a contract photographer for National Geographic and has taken the photographs for two of their books: *The Pacific Crest Trail* and *Still Waters/White Waters*. For *National Geographic* magazine he has done articles on Newfoundland, Yellowstone, Ontario, and eastern Long Island. For the German magazine *Geo* he did a color essay, "Peyote Vision." Portfolios of his photographs have appeared in *Camera* and *Nautical Quarterly*. He has been guest lecturer on photography at Ohio University and is associated with the Maine Photographic Workshop. He has had one-man shows in the U.S. and Canada. Married to Denise Myers, he lives in Crozet, Virginia.

"I came to the Noatak River at the conclusion of a year's continuous canoeing. My partner Ron Fisher and I had paddled some of the better known wilderness waters in the lower forty-eight states. But it is difficult to be prepared for the Noatak: it is an engulfing wilderness watershed, barely touched by man throughout its gradual fall from the Brooks Range to its mouth at Kotzebue Sound, 435 miles downstream. Ron remembers that "our days there passed in solemn beauty." And now the effect of this vast, silent valley on us seems permanent: it is the place we most talk of, and long to return to."

Dan Budnik: The Upper Hudson

Dan Budnik was born on Long Island, New York, in 1933. He studied painting at the Art Student's League, where he became interested in photography. After two years in the army, he began a career in photojournalism. Budnik has taken photographs for most of the leading international magazines and for TIME-LIFE Books.

"At the age of six I robbed my piggy bank and cut school, venturing twenty-five miles into New York City to view the Hudson frozen solid—'an event of the century,' said the morning radio newscaster. All day long, for a nickel, I rode a railroad passenger ferry back and forth across the river to New Jersey, plowing through the thickest ice I had ever seen. The captain gave me cups of hot tea and a seat near the coal stove in his cabin, but, best of all, he gave me my first account of the upper Hudson, a wild and wondrous place with a tiny drop of a lake where the Hudson was born each day like the sun. That winter's day I was officially listed a 'missing person,' a designation I now regard as meaning 'one with the Hudson.' Years later a magazine assignment would enable me to explore the entire Hudson watershed, leaving me with a lasting love of the place where a river is born.

"The present state of the Hudson River symbolizes all American rivers, and through continued misuse, their common destiny. Pure at its source, it is fearfully polluted before it empties into the sea; yet paradoxically, it remains a source of poetic

inspiration. This dichotomy has fostered within me a conflict between love and anger; it has led me to photograph the Hudson for more than a dozen years. This is my river, and I have learned to cherish Old Father Hudson. I wish that I could protect him as well."

Annie Griffiths: The Boundary Waters

Annie Griffiths is a free-lance photographer living in Minneapolis. She graduated from the University of Minnesota with a B.A. in photojournalism. She has contributed to several National Geographic Society books and articles.

"The Boundary Waters/Quetico park is an international wilderness separated only by one hundred miles of a waterways border. Photographing in such an area is a joy. One can paddle from picture to picture, drink freely from the clear glacial streams, and sleep beneath the grandest white pines left in the United States."

Wendell Metzen: The Suwannee

Wendell Metzen is a Florida-based photographer specializing in natural history. His work appears in many publications, including National Geographic, National Wildlife, and Sierra Club calendars.

"At times a dark forbidding place, when shrouded by fog, it can be as mysterious as a Scottish Loch. As the sun rises, it is a most beautiful cathedral in which to meditate, in mid-day hot and lazy, and at sunset a glorious explosion of color before a darkness full of life. The Suwannee River that I know is not just one place but a whole world.

"For over seven years now, the Suwannee has provided me with a special place for frequent retreat where I can observe the flow between the animal and plant life. The camera serves as a tool for interacting with and interpreting these life processes."

Yva Momatiuk and John Eastcott: The Atchafalaya

Yva Momatiuk and John Eastcott, a well known wife-and-husband team, regularly take on photographic assignments in the wilderness areas of the world. She was born in Warsaw, Poland, earned an architecture degree and edited a magazine in that field. A New Zealander, he received a degree in photographic arts in London. His photos of the Arctic were published in Great Slave Lake Blues. Their work together has appeared in a number of other books, including Wild Places and Wild Shores of North America. Several of their photo-essays for National Geographic magazine won prizes for excellence.

"Photographing the Atchafalaya Swamp in Southern Louisiana was like chasing butterflies in tall grass. It demanded patience, gave joy, and affected all senses. Our eyes learned to see many shades of green in the gobelins of the aquatic forest; our ears tuned in on splashing fish, gliding cottonmouths, and hunting racoons. The sense of smell disclosed stagnant, boggy pools and wet hollows overgrown with luxuriant

blossoms. The skin grew accustomed to the humid, heavy air, the black oily mud, and omnipresent insects. And the taste? What was the taste of the Atchafalaya? It came in Cajun and Creole dishes of teal, crawfish, catfish, crab, and oyster mushrooms. Thus the swamp nourished us in her many ways."

David Muench: The Colorado and Rio Grande

David Muench, a Californian, attended several universities before studying photography at the Art Center School of Design in Los Angeles. Known for his striking portrayals of the Western landscape, he is totally involved in "recording the spirit of the land." As he further describes it: "To photograph in nature allows me to retain a childlike pattern of discovery and to communicate to people the same impressions and feelings I experience. Hopefully my work leads to a celebration of man and the earth—and the mystical forces of nature which help to shape our destinies." He has published some fifteen books including Desert Images, Arizona, and Colorado. In 1975 he was commissioned to provide photographs for 33 large murals on the Lewis and Clark Expedition for Jefferson Expansion Memorial in St. Louis, Missouri. He has taught photography, and his one-man shows have been held in galleries on the East and West coasts.

"Personally, aside from the thrills and hectic action associated with rapids and river running on these waterways, I find myself overwhelmed, awed, creativity heightened and challenged in the big canyons of the Colorado and the Rio Grande. Contrasts of subtlety and enormity—silence and time—challenge the mind's eye. The canyon's blend of stone and silence, space and time, are for me an intensified sense of awareness to the great things around me.

"Within the canyons the flow of waters has the free spirit I imagine these great rivers once had before man controlled them. This sense of their freeness is very important to me."

Boyd Norton: The Salmon

Boyd Norton spent nine years as a nuclear physicist for the Atomic Energy Commission in Idaho near the Salmon River. Ten years ago he gave up science to become a free-lance photographer and writer specializing in nature, wilderness preservation, and environmental problems. He is the author of six critically acclaimed books, including Snake Wilderness, Rivers of the Rockies, and Wilderness Photography. His photographs and articles have appeared in such leading magazines as Audubon, Popular Photography, and National Geographic. In 1980 he received an award from the Environmental Protection Agency for his "exciting environmentally related writing and photography." He currently lives in Colorado where he established an environmental education organization, the University of the Wilderness.

"The Salmon. My Salmon River. Yes, it's true. I feel very possessive about this country. I've made thirty, maybe forty trips on the Salmon and Middle

Fork of the Salmon and, even though I've run many other rivers, I keep coming back here. Why? There's something about this Salmon River wilderness. It's a gentle wilderness, soft and welcoming, with no harsh edges. Yet, at the same time it's among the most remote and rugged country this side of Alaska. And the river itself: wild, untamed, and—in places—gentle, too. Maybe it's the challenge of running Salmon Falls, Bailey Creek, Elkhorn, and other rapids. There's one rapids, however, which is mine: Big Mallard. Perhaps it's also my nemesis. We have this battle, Big Mallard and I. Usually I'm on the brink of disaster, out of control in the raging waves, heading toward that big rock just left of center, pulling on the oars for all I'm worth and barely escaping each time, bouncing madly through the tail waves, looking back to see what I just missed and feeling high on that hot, coursing jolt of adrenaline. That's a part of what the Salmon and the Middle Fork of the Salmon are all about.

"I'll be back. And maybe next time I'll make a perfect run through Big Mallard."

George Silk: The Buffalo

George Silk, a New Zealander by birth, left his native land in 1939 as a war photographer for the Australian government. He then began 30 years of work on LIFE magazine, 1943–73, which led him into the world of outdoor sports, particularly sailing. It was a natural next step to aim his camera at the sea and the land, and to capture their bold shapes and colors on film. From there he branched to nature photography — animals, birds, and things environmental. He has won many awards, including the American Society of Magazine Photographers' Award of the Year (1964). His work was exhibited in the "Family of Man" show at the Museum of Modern Art in New York as well as in other major museums.

"When I first glimpsed the Upper Buffalo through sleet and the gloom of a late winter evening, I was depressed. The sullen-looking gray water overflowing the banks was trying to drown the alders, and only the occasional twang of a branch springing free gave a sign of survival. Astride the river, battleship-gray rocks, used to this annual onslaught, stood unyieldingly. Everywhere on the gentle hills above the river a gray lifeless forest oppressed the senses.

"In the next few days, the sun warmed the rocks, the sap flowed and the spirits lifted as spring flecked the landscape. What a marvellous three weeks of photography!

"Later, the charm lessens as the river dries up and snakes reclaim their territory."

Charles Steinhacker: The Allagash

Charles Steinhacker — photographer, author, teacher — is the director of Nature Photography of America. A New Yorker, educated in the east at Dartmouth and New York University, he now lives in Jackson Hole, Wyoming, but returns to the Allagash region in the summer. He is well known for his three large format books: Superior: Portrait of a Living Lake, Yellowstone: A Century of the Wilderness Idea, and The Sand Country of Aldo Leopold. His ability to communicate what he knows is considered to be rare indeed, and this facility has placed him in great demand as a teacher and lecturer at colleges and universities, environmental groups, and outdoor organizations. He has been the recipient of numerous grants, fellowships, and prizes, and his work has appeared in many of our leading magazines.

"I first saw the Allagash in 1951 as a member of Camp Wanderlust, a seven-week canoe trip through the wilderness of northern Maine. In a sense it was my 'basic training': the mosquitoes, black flies, and 'no-see-ums' were enough to break a young boy's will. Yet, I returned three years in succession, finally as official 'fishing counselor.'

"My appreciation of the Allagash in those days consisted of a desire to catch every trout in the state of Maine. But as my sensibilities and values evolved, I was drawn back to the Allagash as a photographer who wanted to use his craft to further the cause of conservation. The Army Corps of Engineers was proposing a dam that would flood a major portion of the Allagash River. With so little wilderness left in the northeastern part of the country, the idea sounded grotesque. I approached the Sierra Club with a plan for a book that might sound the alarm on what we were about to lose. The proposal was accepted, and together with a brand new bride, I headed up to Maine.

"My wife's initial act as a 'camping lady' was decisive. Hooking the first trout of her life, she stood up suddenly in the canoe and effortlessly deposited all of my cameras on the bottom of Allagash Stream. This placed me at a distinct disadvantage. Also, I had begun to notice that the pervasive green and blue of the area in the summertime severely limited the potential for color photography. I vowed to return in the fall.

"My memories of the Allagash can be distilled into two basic sounds: the call of the loon versus the whine of the chain saw. Eventually the Allagash was designated a 'State Wilderness Waterway,' and the need for a book evaporated. The loon had won a reprieve. And for fifteen years my pictures remained waiting for publication.

"A final irony: today, after all these years, 'they' are still trying to get a dam built—this time on the even wilder St. John River. That's the secret of their success: they never quit!"

Steve Wilson: The Fraser

Steve Wilson studied fisheries at the University of Washington, photography at Los Angeles' Art Center and is now a director of the ENTHEOS group. Three active beaver lodges lie within a hundred feet of his home on Washington State's Kitsap Peninsula; in the winter, female trout dig their redds (nests) under his cantilevered porch and spawn. He mulches the garden and orchard with pond weed and water lilies and pays taxes by being the "human member of a business partnership that includes hundreds of wild animals from leech and earthworm to river otter and cougar — the animals' participation is photographic cooperation beyond reason and mine is the making and selling of photographs of them. It is a commensal arrangement I have practiced for twenty-five years." It works — as perhaps was intended several billion years ago.

"Man is not a parasite upon the Fraser River. He has not dammed it. He has not channeled it. He has not polluted it. The Fraser is still a serious, major river and in my part of the continent there aren't many left. When my forebears were choking up the "mighty Columbia," turning her into a series of silting basins, stair-stepping their dammed way into our continent, the Canadians opted for natural rapids and aeration rather than navigation, for fish rather than hydro-power, for purity rather than sewage, radiation, and industrial wastes … and I thank the Canadians.

"I've driven, hiked, floated, and swum many a happy, frigid Fraser mile. I still laugh about a short hike through the bush, years ago. I had heard that migrating salmon were milling about by the hundreds in a hole on the middle reaches of the watershed. There wasn't an acre of water more than two feet deep within fifty miles; but I was going to have a long and leisurely look at salmon behavior so I took my scuba tanks and was crashing through the underbrush in my wet suit when I encountered a couple of Canadian Fisheries biologists working their way back to the road. They confirmed that there were hundreds of salmon ahead, but as they pushed on I heard, in a dumbfounded voice, 'That guy sure must get into rivers.' I do!!"

Index